OWN THAT GUY IN 60 DAYS

OWN THAT GUY IN 60 DAYS

A Practical Guide to Love for the 21st Century Woman

By Blake Lavak

Foreword by Dr. Imara Hurlingham, DClinPsy

DURHAM PRESS
FLORIDA

Published in 2014 in the United States by Durham Press, Florida

CIP information on file at the Library of Congress

Library of Congress Control Number 2014939670

Lavak, Blake, 1961-

ISBN 978-0-9961023-1-5

eBook ISBN 978-0-9961023-0-8

Printed in the United States of America

First Paperback Edition

Cover by PO'R Designs

www.ownthatguyin60days.com

Dedicated to my father, the quintessential English gentleman, who taught me the importance of original thought, and to my mother, who supported my efforts to think that way.....

GALATIANS 6: 7-9 (KJV)

7: Be not deceived; God is not mocked: for whatsoever a man soweth, that shall he also reap.
8: For he that soweth to his flesh shall of the flesh reap corruption; but he that soweth to the Spirit shall of the Spirit reap life everlasting.
9: And let us not be weary in well doing: for in due season we shall reap, if we faint not.

Foreword

"Own that Guy in 60 Days" is quite unlike any of the dating self-help books currently on the market. It offers a fresh new perspective on the age old problem of dating. Rather than being written by "experts by training" who shroud their advice in complex dating and psychological theories, Blake Lavak has written an informative book from the unique position of an "expert by experience". This subtle change in author position, results in a potent and compelling book which is based on his own dating experiences, observations and interpretations.

Blake captures the attention of the reader from the start, by writing in an honest, open and humorous way about his dating experiences and observations. He presents a book which is thought provoking, stimulating and motivating. He shares the dating strategies and methods which have been tried and tested by women throughout the ages and brings them to life through four women he considers to be skilled at the dating game.

The book challenges prevailing dating advice, which suggests that women take a passive, rather than active, approach to dating. In his book, Blake directly addresses the modern day woman's basic confusion which arises from mixed social messages regarding feminism and masculinity. Modern women are encouraged to be masculine in business which equates to being bold, brave and direct, and feminine in their romantic life which equates to being passive, docile, amenable and patient.

Blake empowers women to have the confidence to use all of their strengths through interactions containing both feminine and masculine traits, to ultimately get and keep the man of their dreams. In a novel approach, Blake presents both the successes and misfortunes associated with employing the dating techniques he describes. This allows the reader to decide for themselves how they may adapt and employ the techniques. Blake suggests that women who are successful are bold, but that they are simultaneously subtle and thoughtful in how they do it.

Some of the techniques Blake describes may appear shocking and provocative, but the psychological and emotional impacts they have on men are real, powerful and long lasting. If practiced, the principles contained within his book will encourage you to proactively engage and connect with the dating process differently. If you are unsatisfied with your current dating experiences and achievements, and want to have a dating experience which ends up with the results you want this is the book for you.

Dr Imara Hurlingham, DClinPsy
April 2014

Introduction

It is remarkable how easy it is to land a great guy just by using the right technique. And yet, so many otherwise capable women struggle in this department. So the question must be asked, what are they doing wrong, and what should they be doing instead. This book provides the answer.

As long as the reader follows the principles laid down here, she will get the man she wants. And she doesn't have to have movie star looks, or a flat stomach, whitened teeth, or bee stung lips. In fact, none of that matters at all, as long as a few simple guidelines are followed instead. Hard to believe? Of course it is, and therein lies the secret to success. It is precisely because so few women really know how to land a big tuna that they end up with little sardines instead. And that means that a small number of women clean up, and land not just one, but often as many big tuna as they can eat, sometimes even more. Why? Because they know the secret. And once you know how it's done, you can do it too. Over and over again. You can take your pick. Try one for size, and if you don't like him, chuck it back, and get another one. Chances are that the tuna that you threw away will do its damndest to get back on your hook again. So if you do it right, you will be literally spoiled for choice. Can you imagine that, wondering what to do, who to choose, from a school of big tuna all competing against each other to get on the end of your hook. Of course you're wondering, what kind of bait do I have to put out there to create such a feeding frenzy, around little old me. And if it has never happened before, how on earth can it happen now. Well, the bait is you, and just because it hasn't happened before, it doesn't mean it can't happen now, or just as soon as you've read this book, absorbed the basic principles, and put them into practice.

These principles work. They work everywhere, and on all men. Why is that, you're wondering. Well, the answer to that is also simple. Men are stupid. No, I don't mean that they aren't intelligent. They're just not very smart when it comes to women. Of course men can be very intelligent. They've run the world for a long time now. But while they've been busy taking over the world, assembling armies, fighting other armies of men to the death, and in recent history either been down a mine excavating coal, or drilling for oil in the Atlantic, or climbing the corporate ladder, all of which has resulted in men dying at an earlier age than women, the female sex has been doing what most women seem to want to do, which is to have babies. So while men are busy killing other men in battle, or killing themselves on the corporate battlefield, women have been quietly getting on with the creation and nurturing of life, and have generally outlived their male partners in doing so. Just check out a typical Florida retirement home. Lots of old ladies in remarkably good health. Where are all the men? Dead and buried, long ago.

Men are stupid when it comes to women. It's the sex and ego thing. Consider the case where a Russian billionaire is dating a Russian supermodel. The girl is six feet tall and stunning. She also happens to be very smart. She knows about serious Russian literature and has travelled the world. While other models were wasting their earnings on cocaine and the high life, she was buying property in Moscow. Quietly stashing her money in inflation proofed assets.

Meanwhile, her Russian billionaire boyfriend is nearly as broad around the waist as he is tall. He is barely five feet tall in his platform shoes. And he is no Johnny Depp. Pictures of the two of them standing side by side look ridiculous.

It is very clear what the game is here. Ugly rich men buy beauty. Beautiful women sell their beauty for money and the things that money can buy.

Is the Russian billionaire smart or stupid? Chances are that when his girlfriend looks into his eyes and swears undying love that he believes her. Why? Because he wants to believe. And that need to believe, and the self-delusion necessary, is what makes an otherwise intelligent and successful man do an incredibly stupid thing. He marries her, even though his inner voice is telling him that she is after his money rather than him, and one or two kids later, she is entitled to half of his fortune.

His need for an ego boost, for sex, and to feel her love makes him stupid.

The fact is that women are smarter than men. They have to be. Generally speaking, women are smaller and physically weaker than men. So they have to make up for their physical inferiority with mental superiority. If they weren't more than a match for men then they would be dying at a younger age than men. Simple. The numbers don't lie. Women live longer than men. There is no better yardstick to determine the winner in the battle of the sexes. Women come out on top. Everywhere.

Now that we've determined that men are stupid, and women are smart, it becomes clear that by being smart about how to play the mating game, the woman will come out the winner.

You might also be wondering why this book has been written by a man and not a woman. Well, it could be written by a woman. But the women I know who already know the secret to landing the big tuna don't seem to be in any real hurry to share their knowledge with their fellow females. Probably because they're too smart for that. Why share the wealth and let the cat out the bag when you can keep the knowledge for yourself, and have a big fat school of big tuna all to yourself. As usual, women are smarter then men. A typical man, if he's successful with the ladies, will want to tell everybody how he does it, what he said, what he did, in mind numbing detail. In contrast, the successful female player keeps her mouth shut, and doesn't give the game away. Which is one of the basic principles used to land the big tuna, but more on that later.

Oh, and by the way, the 60 days thing...if you take the advice as laid down in this book then you will absolutely own the guy you want at the end of the second month of dating. If you don't then you haven't followed the principles for landing the big tuna. This is not the type of thing where you can pick and choose what you will or won't do. If you decide to do that then it will not work. Chances are that you will read something here and say there's no way in the world that I'm going to do that, or you'll say to yourself that the advice you read here is different from every piece of advice that you've ever been offered before. Maybe a friend or friends will say that's crazy, do what?

Well ask them, and yourself, how things are working out by using all the standard advice offered in the various magazines targeted at women. And books about the so-called rules. These things were generally all written by women. And do your homework on the people who have written all this stuff and you'll see that they evidently aren't taking their own advice, because most of them are single. It's either that, or else their advice is not worth the paper it is written on.

The fact is that if you want to stand out from the crowd then you have to do something different. Sure, you can take the easy way out and wait for the big tuna to spot you and approach you and do the initial work. But you will have to do some work to land him. Use the wrong techniques and he'll be gone. No reason given. Just history. And you'll be wondering where it went wrong, what you did or didn't do that he didn't like. And with no feedback it will be hard to do better next time. Oh, and while you're waiting for him to approach you, your competition might be getting the jump on you because she's following the principles in this book instead of you.

How about just sitting back and letting the big tuna find you? After all, isn't that the way it's supposed to happen? Cute girl waits for her Prince Charming to pull up next to her, take one look, fall instantly in love, and then provide security and lifestyle for the rest of her life, right? Two words. Dream on.

You get out what you put in. Make no effort apart from applying some make-up and wandering down to your local pick-up joint, and guess what, you'll meet Joe Nobody. But if you apply yourself, make a serious effort, the rewards will soon be yours.

So it really is up to you. As J Pow, the Cambodian philosopher once said to me, "everything can change".

If you read this book and use the techniques then you'll not only land the big tuna, but you'll be able to pick the best of the bunch, and you will own him in 60 days. So let's get started...

1. Where Big Tuna Swim

The first rule about catching a big tuna is that you have to drop your hook in waters where these big fish swim. Sounds obvious, doesn't it. But you would be shocked at how many women literally waste their time and talent at events or places where the sardines congregate, instead of the big tuna.

If you are going to go to all the trouble to get your game plan in order, then you want to execute and make it all worthwhile. And the funny thing is that it is no more difficult to operate successfully in a target rich environment than it is where the pickings are slimmer. In fact, it is easier. There are more targets, and if you are doing it right, then the targets will be competing against each other for your attention, and not just the other way around.

So, figure out what you want. Are you focused on looks, or are you focused on wealth. Maybe you want a young, toned and honed sexual Olympian, or maybe you want a man with a Chelsea townhouse and an underground parking lot for your

Chelsea tractors. Whatever it is that you want, you can find it far more easily if you go where that variety of tuna swim.

Once you have decided what you want, then it is time to do some research. You will find academics in and around universities, and bankers in certain districts of the bigger cities, and athletes anywhere that sport occurs. Should be obvious, but again, lots of women get all dolled up for a night out on the town, hoping to meet the one, and then are disappointed when it doesn't happen, and wonder what went wrong, when all they did was head out with their girlfriends to the same old place they've been to in the past, with the same poor results.

The process of figuring out where the big tuna swim is not hard at all. I have often found myself standing in a pub in southwest London, watching a big international football match, and realized that the guy next to me is a very well known and wealthy actor. Good looking, debonair, well spoken, and single. Sometimes he has a cute young girl with him, but often not. The shocking thing is that there are so few women in there competing for his attention. In fact, he looks ripe for the taking. So where are the women and why are they not in the same pub at the same time?

They are probably heading for some fancy new bar that they read about in a magazine. Instead of doing some homework and finding out where this big tuna lives. Information that is readily available on the internet. It takes about three minutes to find out where this guy lives with a little Google. And about three minutes to learn also that he likes football. And everybody already knows that he likes girls, so that's not a problem.

So, I am confused. One of the most eligible men in London is standing in a bar next to me, and there is hardly a woman in spitting distance. Well here is a little idea for you. Spend a little less time looking for the big tuna on catch.com and a little more time doing your homework on the fish that really exist. The information about these guys is all out there in the public domain, and it doesn't take a rocket scientist to work out that if the Big Tuna lives in a big tuna house in a wealthy part of London, and that if he likes football, that it stands to reason that he will visit the pubs nearby showing the big games on a regular basis.

Work. Research. Focus.

Connect the dots.

You can do it.

If your idea of a big tuna is a beach blond surfer then you won't find him in Oklahoma unless you happen to be very lucky. But if you are willing to do some homework on the best surf spots, the places that the surfers really go to surf, and then read up on surf forecasts, and get there a day or so before the big waves are supposed to arrive, then you are half way to spotting the school of tuna that you'll be fishing for.

Notice that I said you need to find the places that the surfers really go to for surf. Don't waste your time on some spot that is all hyped up and the real surfers avoid. And similarly, don't waste your time standing in a queue to get into some recently opened hotel bar unless you are after a middle aged married man who happens to be in town on a business trip and read the same piece of hype as you.

If you can stand back and see the big picture, work out what type you want, then work out where that type is likely to be, then you are already well on your way to a big catch.

2. Change a Losing Game Plan

A losing game plan will result in a loss. That is a fact. A loss of energy, opportunity, and time. Time, my friends, is not on your side. Unless you make it work for you instead of against you.

How many times are you going to go to the same lame parties full of losers, the same nightspots full of women with a past and men with no future. After a while you start to think and then believe that the stories you read about in supermarket magazines are fantasy. You start to think that the people you see living the high life in those reality shows don't really exist, that it just can't happen, and that even if it does, that it can't happen to you.

The funny thing is that it can happen to you. But you have to believe it and you have to do your best to make it happen.

The first part of making the dream come true is to be realistic about your current situation. If you live in a two horse town where the biggest tuna would hardly feed a family of mice, then you need to think seriously about moving, and fast.

If your sports club is full of lots of younger and hotter women, and you are hoping to eat tuna for dinner, then cancel your membership and join a new sports club. If the pub you go to is full of men who are twenty years older than what you are looking look for then start going to another pub. If the neighbourhood that you live in is dull then look for a new area to cruise, a place where you are much more likely to meet a suitable target, and go there, even if it means a long drive or a train and a bus ride.

Sounds obvious, doesn't it. But let me tell you, I know lots of women who keep doing the same thing, going to the same places, over and over again, and yet they are surprised when they meet nobody worth meeting or nobody at all. I know a super attractive lady with a fancy house and lifestyle, paid for courtesy of a divorce from a wealthy guy, who complains non stop about the lack of eligible men around her. When I suggest that she looks a little further afield than her kids' soccer games, her kids' school parking lot, lunch with her girlfriends, dinner with her mother, work-outs with her brother, she looks at me with a vacant expression. I mean, what the heck, does she really expect to meet her next big tuna at any of those so-called events. You have got to be kidding.

Despite all the evidence to the contrary, she will not meet the type of guy she is looking for unless she makes a change to her game. And if she can't even meet the right type of guy, then she has zero chance of landing him.

It's a numbers game. Simple. And it takes work. Don't expect to get something for nothing. A famous sportsman said, when it was suggested to him that his success was down to a lot of luck, "the harder I work the luckier I get".

There was a man who was very successful at attracting beautiful and intelligent women, all of them invariably much younger than him. He didn't flash the cash, and he didn't lavish praise or affection, or swear undying love. But he worked hard at it. He joined internet dating sites and put the effort in, meeting countless numbers of available women before selecting a few. His friends were amazed and envious as he showed up with one attractive woman after another, and told stories about his sex life that seemed scarcely believable. It was ninety nine percent down to effort, and one percent luck.

So the harder you work at it, the luckier you will get.

And as you learn to play the game, you will get better at it too. You should expect to make some mistakes along the way. But the mistakes will teach you very valuable lessons, as long as you consider the reality of the situation rather than consoling yourself with the comfort of delusion. You might say too much or talk too much about yourself. This is a big mistake. But also one that is easy to make, before you improve your game and learn what to say and what not to say. But again, more on that later.

Positioning is a very important part of the process of getting what you want. You can't own that man until you've found him. So think about what you want, think about where a man like that can be found, and change your habits so that you put yourself in the place he is more likely to be. Keep working at it until you get it right, be prepared to admit mistakes, and keep changing your game plan until it is working for you. The world is a big place full of an awful lot of people. It is also full of an awful lot of awfully unsuitable people, and you can't afford to waste time and effort there when there is always another opportunity around the corner. So if it isn't working, then change. Make the effort and keep making the effort.

On many occasions I've been surrounded by extremely eligible young men, all earning a lot of money, with great academic and professional pedigrees. And they were all looking for a nice girlfriend. Their problem was the same as yours, meeting someone suitable.

As it happens, big tuna like these are busy people. They usually have demanding jobs that take up a lot of time and energy. And at the end of the day they normally head out to a local bar and have a few drinks with their buddies.

Find out where these people work and hang out.

Your goal has got to be to put yourself in the water that is absolutely teeming with big tuna. Of course, you have to determine for yourself exactly what type of tuna you like best. But whatever that type is, find out where it lives, works, and recreates, and get yourself there.

And then let the games begin.

Before you can do this, it is important to embrace the concept of change as you would a long lost friend. Change is hard. Your brain is hard wired to resist change. Your brain makes you feel very uncomfortable as soon as you start to do something new, so don't be surprised to feel this way once you get on to your new road. But if you stick with it, the new road will start to feel comfortable, and after a little while, you will know this new road like the back of your hand. And a little while after this happens you will feel liberated, and excited.

So if your current game plan isn't delivering the goods, then be brave and make a change.

3. Targets

If you have taken the message from the last chapter, and have left the small pond full of small fish behind, and have now found yourself a bigger pool full of bigger tastier fish, then it is time to identify and then focus on a few targets. A few targets? Absolutely. Remember that it's a numbers game. And if you play the numbers game then you increase your chances of success exponentially.

Remember that there are many reasons why a decent looking target is not worth a second effort. He could be gay, or in love with another person, or homeless, penniless, unemployed, a mama's boy, weak, stupid, pathetic, uninteresting, pathologically dishonest, humourless, bad in bed, smelly, ill, or even diseased. The list is endless. And because people rarely, if ever, are upfront about their worst attributes, it takes a while before you figure them out.

So given that lots of good looking prospects are in fact very bad prospects, it pays to put all your eggs in a bunch of baskets instead of putting them all in one. Now the romantics out there will be saying that they want to be in love, and that it should just happen, and that if they happen to fall in love with a guy who just happens to be an unemployed mama's boy who's bad in bed, then it doesn't matter because they're in love. How pathetic. Life is hard so why make it harder than it has to be. By all means fall in love. But it shouldn't be the driver. If it happens then it is a bonus. But the aim here is to get the guy to fall in love with you, not the other way around.

Playing the field has other benefits. The fact is that human beings are competitive by nature. And if your big tuna target thinks he has some competition, then it can work to your advantage. Notice that I said "thinks" he has competition. I did not say "knows" he has competition. The last thing you want to do is let your target know that there is another guy on the scene. But let him suspect that it might be true. If questioned about it, do not answer truthfully. All is fair in love and war.

More importantly, you need to increase your chances of landing the big tuna, and you do that by having more than one baited hook in the water, working for you, at the same time. Yes, it means more work tending the lines. Which in real terms means keeping things going with daily texts, emails, phone calls, and dates.

This is a business, after all. If you do this and do it right, then it will pay off handsomely.

And if you get a little practice then it gets easier and easier.

So play the field, but be sure to keep the tuna you are after well away from each other. They should not be in the same pool. They should not even know that there is another pool where you go fishing.

This guideline is not without its risks. If you are unlucky enough to be found out then the game is over with these tuna and it means starting over again. So you must make sure that there is no chance that the tunas cross paths and discover that you have been fishing with two or more rods at the same time.

The most effective way to ensure that this does not happen is to keep everything about each tuna separate from one another. Do not introduce more than one tuna to your friends or family until you have him hooked and ready to be grilled. You can not control what these friends and family might say, and the chances are that they will let the cat out of the bag, inadvertently. When this happens it happens fast and with calamitous results. If you tell one tuna that you are going on holiday to Malta with your parents, and you go there with another tuna, then you better make sure that it never comes up in conversation between the second tuna and your folks, or else you are in big trouble.

So the only real way to safeguard against getting caught is to ensure that your tuna targets do not meet each other, your friends, or your family.

This might sound impossible, but it is easier than you think. The easiest way is to imply that you don't have a lot of friends, or that you don't see your family very often. But don't go into details. As for where you are all the time when you aren't with him, there is always the gym, working late, going to bed early, not feeling too well, out with a girl friend who has relationship issues, out with a gay guy friend, out with an old friend from school catching up. If you put your mind to it you can find many excuses for time spent tending to other tuna. Keep any explanation short and sweet. If you play the game along the guidelines outlined here then he won't care, and will probably be pleased that he has you all to himself, or so he thinks.

4. The Love Balance

Landing the big tuna requires that you get this guy to fall madly in love with you. If he doesn't fall, and fall hard, then you have failed in your mission. You have done something wrong. You may have done many things wrong. Or you might have fallen in love with him first, and harder. Oh dear, this will never do.

Remember that the person who loves the least has the control. Sad but true. And think about examples of couples you know where one person has had an affair. And when the affair was over the couple got back together. And lived happily ever after. Doesn't happen that way too often does it. Why not. Because what actually happens is counter intuitive. Let's say Mary cheats on Mark. They get back together and Mary says sorry and never does it again. She feels guilty and is as nice as pie forever more and never ever even glances at another guy. It should happen this way, because otherwise why would she get back together with Mark. What actually happens is that Mary ends up in the position of power, because she cheated and got caught. It will be Mark who makes the extra effort and not Mary. And the reason is that Mark will be worried that if it happened once then it will happen again. And unless he finds a way to take the power back, it will happen again, given an opportunity.

The point of this little story is to illustrate the importance of control. Fall madly head over heels in love, by all means. But make sure that he loves you more. That way you have the control. And if you are the one in control then you run the show and get what you want, and he'll be eager to please, not just today or tomorrow, but for as long as you want. Want a bigger house. He'll provide it. Want a nicer vacation. He'll provide that too. Want a bunch of kids. No problem. Get the love balance the wrong way and you'll be sitting at home by yourself while he's out having a few beers with the boys after work. Or that's what he'll tell you. And then you'll start calling him and telling him to come home, the rot will set in, and he'll be off with another woman who loves him less but sees him more.

So the plan is to have a good look at a number of prospects, and to remember to fall in love, but to make sure from the outset that the big tuna falls harder for you. Romance is good. Love is great. The more the merrier. But the balance absolutely must be in your favour. Forget that and you are doomed. No control. No power. No getting what you want. And you hand him everything.

You are no doubt wondering how on earth you manage to fall in love, but make sure the big tuna falls for you harder. The answer is mental strength, some people seem to be blessed with it, and others have to work for it instead. The fact is that mental strength can be developed, so if you're a little weak in this department, it can change. You just have to think about it a little and then take little steps in the direction you want to go, so that over time you get smarter and stronger. Just like going to the gym. You go once or twice and don't see any difference. But after twenty visits you start to notice that you can lift more weights, run faster and longer, and you feel better. You feel more alive. You feel more confident. You feel more attractive. And that new strength and confidence makes you much more attractive to your targets. Which makes it easier to keep the love balanced in your favour.

Ideally, you really want this guy to fall for you while you give him the illusion that you are in love with him too. This gives you all the power and all of the control. You want to get him wrapped around your little finger so that he does as he is told.

Always keep it in mind as you play this game that it is essential to keep control of your emotions. If you get a sense that the balance of love is skewed in his favour and not yours, then the game has changed. While you may still land the big tuna, it will be on his terms and not yours.

So make sure that the set of love scales is always leaning your way. And if the balance is the wrong way, then take steps to fix it fast. You will learn how to do that a little later in the book…so if it happens don't despair!

5. Going Fishing

You aren't going to catch anything sitting at home watching reality TV. So why not get out there and make your own reality more interesting than anything the digital media world has to offer.

The women who are really good at this game treat it like a business. And of course, it is. And there is a lot to play for. Land the big tuna and you can be set up for life. Everything you want. And no need to study hard to get good grades to get into a good university to get a good job so you can earn a lot of money to buy things you want. Nope. There's a far easier and fun way. Land the big tuna and piggy back off all the hard work he did to get the good life. And it can be a lot of fun landing the big tuna. Wining and dining, fun parties, exotic vacations, gifts. Sounds a lot better than studying for exams and job interviews and annual reviews. Amazingly, men of the big tuna species seem to be so busy working hard that they fail to observe the simple fact that they are doing all the work while their beloved partner does no work at all. Simply amazing. I know of one couple where the husband beats his brains out daily trading commodities with other peoples' money while his wife sits at home and spends her days with extremely expensive interior designers who easily talk her into spending $10,000 for a cushion in addition to their

$35,000 monthly consultancy fee. People say that the husband is very clever and the wife is a bit dim. I'd say that she knows her craft very well and obviously has no need for a copy of this book.

My mother would tell you that in her day women only went to university so they could meet a man with good prospects. Meaning, a man who could get a high paying job and keep her in the manner to which she wanted to become accustomed. Have things really changed that much. It seems that women like working, for a while. And then the instinct that they were born with kicks in and they do what comes naturally and start looking around for a provider. Nothing wrong with that at all. Perfectly sensible too. And smart. Land the big tuna, guarantee provision for yourself and children, and then anything goes after that.

Back to the project at hand. Of course it can be an effort to head out looking for love after a hard day at work, but hey you reap what you sow. Why not go out straight from work. You've done your homework, and you know where to go. You're trying a new place. And you have a back-up in case the first place isn't too promising. And you will be brutal if the place or people aren't working for you. Just up and out. Move on to the next venue and to the next new opportunity. Do not waste time is an important rule here. A good fisherman scours the sea looking for tell-tale signs that the water under his boat has lots of big fish. In the old days he would look for birds hovering above the water and head over fast to throw in his hook, because he knew that the birds were there to eat the small fish that had been driven to the surface by the big fish below. Nowadays, fishermen use sonar so that they can actually see the fish from above. No birds or no sonar blips mean no fish, so they take off immediately. You've got to do the same.

At this time it is probably worth mentioning that an unwanted by-product of the go fishing a lot technique is the attention you will get from the sardines. Just as the fisherman curses the small fry who race to his bait and hook themselves, so must you discourage attention from the wrong type of fish. Being nice and talking to sardines will discourage big tuna from approaching you, and it will not be possible for you to take an active approach towards them. Be firm, or be rude, if necessary. But get rid.

Now that we have established that you have to go fishing on a regular basis if you want to catch a big tuna, the question is how one defines regular. The simple answer is that the more practice you put in the better you'll get. If you go out once a week for a year then you've maybe notched up fifty two outings. And if it takes a dozen outings before you get into your swing and start to make it work, and then another dozen to make mistakes and learn from them, then it means a six month learning process before you get productive. Not bad, perhaps. But at this rate you'll probably be about to give up, blame me, and curse the day you bought this book. We all only live once, so why not slot it into top gear and go for it harder.

You should be going out fishing at least four times a week. If not, then you simply aren't taking this seriously. Play your favourite sport once or twice a week and guess what. At the end of the year you'll be about as good as you were at the beginning of the year. Play three times a week and you'll improve a little. Play four times a week and you'll improve a lot. Play six times a week, with application and reflection, rest on the seventh, and you'll be the best that you can be. Put what you will learn from this book into practice every time you go out and you will be awesome and irresistible.

6. See and be Seen

Unless you have eyes in the back of your head, there is no way you should ever sit facing the wall. Sounds obvious, doesn't it. But next time you go out, take a look around you. In a popular pub in London, I routinely see tables of girls all sitting down together enjoying some wine and banter. Guess what. Half the girls are sitting with their backs to the wall but the other half get to look at the wall and their friends who are checking out the action behind them.

By making sure that you are looking at the action you win two ways. You get to see the tuna and the tuna get to see you. The girls who are looking the wrong way just handed a huge advantage to their more intelligent and opportunistic friends.

Next time be smart and make sure that you sit or stand somewhere so that you can see and you can be seen. Otherwise you aren't trying. You're better off at home on the sofa with the proverbial DVD and glass of red wine.

Let's say the only table they have available is at the back, buried behind a small jungle of plants or behind a partition wall. Or downstairs where there is no bar, no atmosphere, no action, and most importantly no opportunity. Forget it. Walk out.

You have got to make the trip worthwhile. Do not allow yourself to get dumped somewhere that is convenient for everyone but you. Sure, the food might be good, and the place might be fashionable, but if it doesn't get you where you want to be then move on. It just isn't worth spending time waiting in a line or making do with a poor spot in a good place when that time could be spent in a place that is happening for you straight away. Contrary to what some people think, big tuna don't only hang out in supposedly famous and popular places. There are lots of big tuna around, they aren't an endangered species, and you can find them in lots of places. But you need to meet them before you can hook them. And that won't happen in a dead beat locale.

So be flexible, and be ready to move. If the place you are in is not conducive to the aim at hand, then adjust your position.

You are trying to get the edge every time you are out. It doesn't mean that you are only focused on one thing. By all means make sure you are out to enjoy yourself and that that will happen even if a tuna doesn't come swimming your way on that particular occasion, but by tweaking a few things like being visible to the tuna, and making sure you can see them when they glide into view, you are working hard and working smart to ensure that you take every chance that might come your way.

Another important tweak is to ensure that you are accessible. A problem with being situated with your back to the wall is that there is inevitably going to be either tables or chairs or people physically in between you and your chosen variety of tuna. This presents a problem because few men are sufficiently confident and skilled to run the gauntlet to get to you through these various obstacles, and if they are then you are probably in way over your head. And that's because if he is that good then he is going to play you and you are not going to play him. This is a dangerous fish of the sea, a shark, and not one to engage in battle with, unless you want to lose, which is almost certainly guaranteed.

So the best way to avoid sharks while fishing for big tuna is to make little runs out into open water, and then to retreat back to the shallows. Make a run, retreat. Wait a while. See and be seen. Then make another run into deep water. Retreat. Do this regularly. Do not sit and wait for the sharks to swim over to you for dinner. For they shall. They'll spot you because you're visible. And nothing will get in their way if they decide to make you their target. An experienced shark will eat you alive. You'll enjoy being eaten. But at the end of the experience you'll be in pieces. At you'll be wondering what happened.

By moving out into open water you are giving the big tuna out there an opportunity to swim up along side you and strut their stuff. And if you don't like what you see, just retreat. Try again a little later. On what pretext you're probably wondering. Easy. Going to the bathroom. Getting a glass of water. Or some ice. Or a slice of lemon, or a napkin. Or to ask for a menu. Keep moving. Make sure you are accessible and then a whole world of opportunity opens up. And it gives you options. And room for opportunities to flourish as more and more tuna suddenly materialize to see what might be on offer. Then when you've had enough, just head back to your seat for a chat with the girlfriends. The tuna will go crazy. You've whetted their appetite and after another little foray or two into open water they'll be ravenous. After a while they'll be working on their best lines, quietly wracking their brains trying to come up with something witty and interesting to say to you to capture your attention. They'll be watching your every move, while pretending not to see you at all, and they will be trying desperately to anticipate your next move into open water, when it will come, why, and in which direction. Will she go to the bathroom, or to the bar, should I wait for her to walk by me or should I approach her. This will all be happening just as long as they get a feeling that there might be something to play for. And that will happen if you move about. Simple.

Remember the rule, make sure you can see and be seen, and make sure you are accessible.

7. Be bold, be Brave

Well if you've got this far and really absorbed the guidelines outlined in the first few sections then it means that you are ready to start getting into the meat of the matter of what it takes to land the big tuna.

You have started to venture out of the shallow water full of sardines, into deeper water where the big tuna swim. You are also now really good at spotting a situation or location for what it is, and therefore knowing when it isn't going to work for you, no matter how long you stay there. And you move on to more fertile locations in a heartbeat. You've also got your guard up, and know that the trick is to find love, but to make sure that when you find it, that the object of the game is to make absolutely certain that the big tuna loves you more than you love him. You're also going out a lot. None of this once a week malarkey. This is a business. And a serious one. And it takes commitment and dedication. And finally, you've now honed your early game to perfection, and when you're somewhere full of big fat tasty tuna, you're making sure that you can see them all, and that they can see you. And you're creating little opportunities all the time for the tuna to sidle up to you and show and tell you what wonderful specimens they are, to sell themselves, and all at their expense.

All of this is helping to create the situation where it all happens. Big tuna sees you, you see him, you bump into each other, and then it all starts to happen. Or should do. But what happens when it doesn't happen.

Sometimes you'll need to add a little something extra into the mix. And why is that you're wondering. The sad fact is that in some parts of the western world men can be a little, well, for lack of a better word, timid. You've got to remember that you ladies can be somewhat intimidating. And this is especially true if you're gorgeous, witty, intelligent, and successful. Then put six or eight of you together, add wine, laughter, and it can all look like an impossible task for a guy to summon up the courage to make a play. First he has to think of something to say, then he has to wander over, and then he has to deliver his opening line, often to an audience as well as to you. Well let me tell you that this isn't easy. Sure, after a bucket of beer he'll be unstoppable, but that is hardly the ticket for you.

A very attractive woman in her mid thirties told me that when she is standing at a bus stop in Paris that every male from the age of eighteen to sixty five hits on her. She gets to London and she is ignored completely. And as a consequence she has virtually no male company, despite her obvious qualities in the looks department.

Then there are stories about developments in Los Angeles which add weight to the argument. Tales whereby men in LA don't even bother approaching women at all. Why. Because the women in LA approach a man if they're interested, otherwise they don't. Everybody there seems to know that this is how it works, and they play by those rules. It saves men a lot of bother. And women choose exactly who they want. So the roles are reversed. There is some evidence that suggests that men in North America and the United Kingdom have become emasculated. That's because divorce is now so prevalent, with over fifty percent of first marriages now failing, and seventy percent of second marriages also failing, and with the consequences of divorce being so severe, financially speaking, that men are towing the line and behaving. But behaving almost too well. They daren't look at another woman, talk to another woman, much less flirt with another one. Terms like emotional cheating have come into being, and women actually harangue their boyfriends and husbands for almost any contact with any woman other than themselves, to the point that a quick click onto a porn site is tantamount to sexual deviance and automatic and instant grounds for a costly divorce.

My how things have changed. When I was a kid I not only relied on my Dad's stack of Playboy magazines, kept supposedly hidden in his closet, to enable me to see what the delicious lumps and bumps on a girl's body actually looked like under her clothes, but it also helped me to understand what I was supposed to do with a female body if I was ever lucky enough to have one to play with.

Roll on to the early part of the twenty first century and now there's something wrong with a guy if he admits to enjoying a little solo sex with the one he loves while sitting in front of a computer screen with all that it has to offer these days. Forty or fifty years ago there was something wrong with the kid who didn't like a sneak peak at a centrefold inside Playboy or Penthouse. Now we're all perverts. Go figure.

So if American and British men have become emasculated, and if the trend in LA where women have adopted the habits of men before they became emasculated spreads to the east coast of America and eventually to London and elsewhere in Europe, then the next guiding principle becomes even more essential to guarantee success with the big tuna.

Be bold.

Sit around and wait for the big tuna to come to you? Forget it. You could be waiting a long time. And lots of perfectly good tuna could just glide by while you're waiting oh so patiently for a nibble.

The famous American author, Mark Twain, said that he only regretted the things he didn't do. John Betjeman, the English poet and writer once said, when asked shortly before he died what he'd do differently if he had his life to live over again, that he'd like to have more sex.

Why wait when it is all there for the taking. If you see something you like then take a chance and try and grab it. You can always let go if it is not to your liking. Instead of looking at a nice looking tuna as it swims by, why not go and bump into it yourself. See what happens. Of course he may be gay or inappropriate for any number of reasons, as we've already discussed, but nothing ventured nothing gained. So when you're out and about, adopt a brave attitude. Don't be afraid to approach a guy. In fact, make a point of approaching every guy who catches your eye. It takes a little practice, but the harder you work at it the better you'll get.

And be ready for a big surprise. You will be shocked at how you'll be received by the guys you a show a little attention to. They will be delighted beyond belief. And why is that you're wondering.

Let me tell you that there isn't a single guy I know who wouldn't be absolutely gobsmacked and blown away if a girl walked up to him out of the blue and introduced herself with a little compliment. And the reason is that it hardly ever happens. Sure, if you're an attractive lady, and if you get out a lot, there's no doubt that you'll get a lot of attention. No doubt also that a lot of that attention will be unwanted. It's the way our society works. Guys are supposed to hit on the girls, and girls are supposed to play hard to get, even when they want the attention and want the guy. And girls are certainly not supposed to play the brazen hussy and make the running. It isn't ladylike. It isn't done. Well think again. You keep letting all the other girls do the ladylike thing. Let them do all the running away with an occasional glance back before running again. And while they're getting on with that, you make sure that you're saying "hi and how are you good looking" to all the fresh tuna that the other girls are running from.

I can guarantee that being bold will pay dividends. How bold is bold you're wondering. How about this as an example of how bold you can be, and the results of such action.

The setting is a popular pub in Notting Hill, a fashionable area of west London. A group of professional guys are heading over there to enjoy a few beers while watching a football match on the widescreen TV. As they walk in and scout the place for a table and chairs for six, one guy notices three girls sitting at a table, two girls facing the wall with the third facing them and the action. Three guys sit down at the only available table, which happens to be next to the girls. They ignore the girls, drink their beer, and watch the game intently. At one point, the girl I call Rock Chick, the one facing the other two girls and the action, tries to chat to the guys, but she is rebuffed, it seems that football comes first. So she waits. A little while later a bigger table nearby becomes available and all six guys sit down together. The game ends and four of the guys go outside for a cigarette. Rock Chick sees her chance, and acts boldly. She stands up, and walks over to her target, the big tuna. She casually and confidently sits down next to the big tuna. She doesn't ask. She just does it. And then she asks the tuna, "don't I know you, aren't you a journalist for the BBC?". He is flattered by the attention, and more than a little surprised. And he's wondering who this girl is and what she wants. She's obviously mistaken him for someone else, and he quickly points this out to her. He explains that he is a banker and not a journalist. She doesn't move. She smiles. She takes a little sip of beer from her glass. Then she leans forward and quietly says to him that she is going to have sex with him that night, but not exactly in those words. And then she leans back and smiles at him again. The guy is incredulous. This has never happened to him before. He's thinking it must be a joke, that his friends are setting him up, and he asks her which of his friends has planned the joke. But of course it is no joke. And that's what she tells him. And so they start talking. But not about sex and not about football.

Rock Chick was bold, and she was brave. The guy she approached was easily the best looking guy in the place. And a highly intelligent and educated man. And married to a woman from a wealthy upper crust family. He had enjoyed a very successful career in finance and belonged to the most exclusive clubs in town. Rock Chick was uneducated, having left school at sixteen, lived in a squalid flat in the suburbs, and had an eighteen month old baby girl, and no career and no prospects. Despite the differences, and before long, he was in love with her. And later on he left his wife to live with her.

This very simple action changed the course of a number of lives. A casual bystander might say that her behaviour was shocking and immoral, and that he should have stayed and not strayed. But the fact is that the guy had been unhappy for years. He and his wife were ill suited. He had started drinking heavily, and his life was going nowhere but down. Rock Chick had been similarly unhappy up until that evening, and her life improved markedly from that point onwards.

Rock Chick didn't wait for the guy to approach her. She saw an opportunity and she went for it. They fell in love with each other and the rest is history. She landed the big tuna, but she had to make the first move.

Moral of the story, be bold and be brave.

I am constantly amazed to see large groups of single women out on the town for the evening, who stick together like glue. They say they can't meet a decent man anywhere, and they're all desperate for romance and lust and to find a decent guy with good prospects, and yet they do almost everything possible to make sure that it doesn't happen. What is the point of getting your appearance just right, finding a good venue where the idea is to have some fun and meet a nice guy, and then give off signals the whole time that say the opposite.

Going out in groups is a bad idea. It puts guys off big time. And the definition of a group is any more than two. If you go out with a girlfriend then you'll work together. You'll give each other support and encouragement. You'll take a chance. Because two girls together means that they'll be honest with each other. More than two and everything changes. Suddenly the competitive and jealousy elements creep into the equation. And if a nice looking tuna swims onto the scene then the inter-girl politics starts. Your girlfriends have now become girl enemies. They'll want the guy for themselves, and if they can't have him they'll work hard to make sure you don't land him either. Misery likes company.

Make sure that when you go fishing for big tuna that you take no more than one girlfriend with you. And then when the opportunity presents itself, grab it with both hands. The bolder and braver you are, the more fish you'll catch.

8. Fun and Smiles

Think about it before you say anything.

And ask yourself if you smile a lot, a little, or not at all.

Chances are, that unless you are a naturally smiley type of person, that you don't smile nearly as much as you think you do. If you do smile a lot then you'll probably know because you will have heard it a million times from friends and family. Take a walk down the street and look at the people coming your way. How many smiles do you see? Probably none would be my guess. And the reason for that is that most people are preoccupied with everyday trials and tribulations. Unless there is a good reason to smile, people don't do it. So it follows that unless stirred into smiling action by an event of some kind, you don't smile.

The funny thing is that the single most attractive feature of any woman, regardless of size, shape, age or colour, is a big happy smile. You all get boob jobs, your teeth straightened and whitened, you buy expensive clothes, spend hours in the gym, and then it all goes to waste because you don't smile.

Put yourself in the shoes of a big tuna. He scouts a room looking for openings and opportunities. He sees a number of attractive girls. Nice figures, nice hair extensions, nice shoes. All deeply engrossed in conversations. All looking serious. And all looking quite intimidating. And then he sees one of you lot with her head back laughing. He looks again and he sees you smiling. He is instantly intrigued. And he is interested. Wonder what she is laughing at, wonder what is making her smile. Hey, she seems happy and she looks like she's having some fun. Hey, I'm here to have fun too. Perhaps we can have some fun together. Hmmmmmm, how do I get over and find something to talk to her about. I want to talk to her now. I want to meet her.

Guess what. All you other girls, with your serious conversations and furrowed brows, he's forgotten you exist. Doesn't matter about your Anya Hindmarch bag or your fancy Loubertins. He wants to meet the girl with the smile, and doesn't care that she's spilled her drink on her top, or her outfit is off tone. He wants to meet The Smiley Girl because she looks happy. And he's hoping that they'll be happy together, hopefully for a very long time.

Next time you go out for the evening set your phone to send you a reminder for about an hour or so later that evening. When the alarm goes off and you look at your phone to turn it off, make sure you read the reminder that says "get the edge over the other girls and keep smiling". And then smile.

Men love happy women. They find them hugely attractive. Even if you aren't happy then learn to fake it. Take an acting class if necessary. But start smiling. You will find that more men gravitate to you, and it will happen immediately. Smiles and laughs. Way more attractive than the best perfume, the sexiest outfit, the best body. Put it all together and you have an almost irresistible combination. Add one more thing and you have the knock out combination. More explosive than a Mike

Tyson right hand uppercut, but what would an average girl know about that. While working on getting your smile going is relatively easy, you just have to think about it, the killer ingredient for success is a rarer quality, but by no means impossible to develop.

Fun.

My brother said to me about an ex-girlfriend of mine, and my ex-wife, "Blake, they weren't fun". He was right. And maybe that is a large part of why they aren't in my life anymore. And it may explain why I asked another girl to marry me, even though I wasn't even remotely physically attracted to her. She was mountains of fun. We are talking Himalayas, not Poconos.

I suspect this girl had always had a good sense of fun in her personality. And she has a great smile too. She puts it all together and she is lethal as a result. Any bar, any pub, any restaurant, any club, any party, anywhere at any time. She rules. Everybody wants to be with her, men and women, old and young. I've seen her convert the most stuck up dinner party full of the most up tight people into an event that people have talked about afterwards for years. And she wasn't even invited. I've seen her change a dull and pretentious bar into a super lively and fun place in less than fifteen minutes. And she did it by being fun. I guess you're wondering what she did. All I can remember is a picture of her dressed in a white Marilyn Monroe dress with red high heeled shoes dragging a middle aged millionaire around on his back, blazer and all, while he managed to keep his glass of red wine upright. And despite this supposed humiliation, he was laughing his head off the whole time he was being dragged by his ankles around the dance floor. Did they kick her out, or him? Hardly. The next time I went in there for a drink the owner approached me and offered me the use of his 65 foot sport fishing boat for the day, any time I wanted it. And he told me to bring the girl along too. That's the power of fun.

There was the other time when I was at a dinner party in Fulham, an affluent part of west London, and it was full of the same old people I met at all the other similarly respectable but boring dinner parties in the area. These parties are peopled by pretentious types all trying to out do each other in the social status game. All pretending to be from terribly important families with breeding going back centuries. In truth, they were pleasant but pretty average in terms of background, hence the pretension and delusion. Half way through the evening I get a text from Fun Girl who says she's nearby and wants to join. Ten minutes later and she's at the table. Ten minutes after that she and I are having a drink while sitting on the floor in the front room adjoining the dining room. Ten minutes after that we're joined by Willy the Snob, who sits down on the floor with us, much to my surprise and amusement. His very well behaved wife is still at the dining table. After three minutes with Fun Girl, Willy has dropped the pretentious manner and behaviour, and wants to have some fun.

Did it matter that Fun Girl is from the wrong side of the tracks, speaks with the wrong accent, dresses like a vamp, and has less than $500 to her name. Absolutely not. Fun Girl is a blast. And within thirty minutes everyone wants to know her and everyone wants to be her friend. The hostess sidles up to me and says, "the girls all really like Fun Girl, and we've decided to invite her into our little group, and we don't do that very often, so can you ask her along to the next dinner party". I thought to myself that they'd never see Fun Girl ever again, and not because she wouldn't be invited to one of their pretentious and boring evenings, but because Fun Girl wouldn't come again, not even if I begged her. Why? Because the other girls weren't fun.

Fun Girl has problems like everybody else. She's had some tough times too. Breast cancer in her mid thirties nearly killed her. And she was raped when she was in her teens. She is not rich, or even financially secure. She lives in a room in a house that she shares with struggling artists. But she manages to keep her problems to herself, and she doesn't let them get her down, and she certainly won't let a problem or two spoil a good evening. And as a consequence, she's very happy, or appears to be, and people gravitate to her as a result. She gets invited to everything, and never has to put her hand in her pocket for a ticket or a place at a dinner table, and she's on every guest list and VIP list going.

She is fun because she is determined to have fun, because she never knows when the party is going to end. And the party for her is life. Perhaps it was the bout with cancer that makes her the way she is. Whatever the explanation is, the end result is very powerful.

We didn't get married. I live in a very small flat and she said that much as she loved me that there simply wouldn't be enough room for all of her shoes. Seemed like a perfectly good reason not to marry someone, so I went away to lick my wounds, and we remain great friends to this day.

Since then, she's been in all of the famous glossy magazines many times, always gracing a celeb party somewhere in London, and she's had many more offers of marriage. She has a great smile, and is lots of fun, and will receive many more marriage proposals, all of the big tuna variety.

If you can smile like her and be half as much fun then you will too.

9. Light as a Feather

Have you seen an episode of The Big Bang Theory? Get a picture of the character called Amy, Sheldon's girlfriend. You don't want to be her.

I am not saying that you need to become an airhead or someone with no depth or substance. Quite the contrary. In fact, you want to be taken seriously and to be respected. And that happens over time as the big tuna gets to know you better. But initially you want to be as light as a feather.

Feathers float around in the air, you are never really sure which way they are going next. They might land in your hand, or they might just as easily fly away on a little gust of wind, never to be seen again.

Be that feather.

When you meet the big tuna, make sure that you keep it light. How light? Very light. No chit chat about your problems or your job. Keep him guessing. And ask him about him. In a light hearted way. Remember that this is not an interview. Well, it is, but you don't want him to think that it is. And whatever he says, and whatever he talks about, your reply should indicate that you have been listening, and that you find him very interesting. But don't reply by telling him your life story. The time for that will come later. Similarly, this is not the time to talk about politics, religion, and your view on birth control or gun control. Do not talk about business deals, family feuds, or ex-boyfriends.

Keep it light.

By letting him talk about himself, which most people love to do, it lets you get the measure of him, and it lets you keep your cards close to your chest, which is where they should be.

Information is power, so why give it away when you can gather it for free.

And when you part ways after your initial contact with him, if you have kept it light and been engaging, he will be intrigued, and will want to see you again. Of course he will want to know something about you, who you are, where you work, but he will also want another chance to talk about himself.

Before he knows it he will be selling to you.

10. Carpe Diem

Regrets, I've had a few, but then again, too few to mention.

Good old Frank Sinatra, he got to the end of his life and he only had a few regrets. Good attitude. Make sure you go for it instead of hanging back and maybe you too will be able to say the same thing in your old age.

Have you ever wondered why some old people are mean and nasty, always in a bad mood, and not fun to be around? And yet some old people are happy and content, and make great company.

I'm pretty sure that the happy old folk are the ones who took their chances, and whether they won or lost, they had a go. They lived their life. They took some chances. Won some, lost some. And at the end of it all they can look back and say well at least I gave it a shot.

The unhappy old folk are the ones who did the opposite. Either they didn't go on that dream vacation when they could, they thought about it a lot but never went, and then they got sick or got arthritis or something, and the moment to live the dream was gone.

Who are you going to be.

Imagine that you win some tickets to a high society polo match. You get there, and suddenly realize that the biggest tuna of all, Prince Harry, is standing nearby.

Do you, glance at him, and glance again, and then wait for him to notice you, or do you gulp down a big glass of champagne and walk over to him and introduce yourself with a big smile.

Be honest.

So you do nothing. Sure, there is no awkward moment, no humiliating rejection, and you get to go home and tell your friends that you were next to Prince Harry, and that you did nothing.

Or, carpe diem, you could walk over and say hello. Although I have never met him, and therefore don't know him, my guess is that he'd be flattered by the attention, and impressed with your confidence. Oh, by the way, if you do get an opportunity like this, remember to be light as a feather.

What is the worst that could happen?

I was with a group of guy friends recently. We were in a pub just off the Kings Road in Chelsea and we were sitting at a table enjoying some male banter over a few drinks. Naturally the conversation was about women. Suddenly one of the guys jumped up and moved quickly to the bar. Strange. We all had drinks because somebody had just bought a fresh round.

He approached the bar and sidled up to an extremely attractive dark haired girl who had just pitched up to buy herself a drink.

He said something to her, she got her drink and went back to sit with her friends. Shot down in flames. Then the walk back to our table for some ribbing.

The fact is that we all respected the guy for having the courage to do what none of us had done, which is to seize the moment and take a chance. You will not be surprised to learn that this guy was the guy in the group who had lots of girlfriends, who wasn't always complaining that he couldn't get a date or find a nice girl. The guy took chances, took rejection on the nose, and picked himself up and then did it all over again.

We wanted to hate him, but he was our hero.

So be that guy too.

A couple of girls that I know were telling me about their recent dating experiences. They had both been on first dates, and they both felt that the dates had gone well, they liked the guys, but then nothing happened afterwards. No follow-up dates. No invitations to dinner or to the movies. They were both flummoxed.

They asked me what had gone wrong, why they hadn't heard from the guys again.

So I asked them if they had called or texted the guy the next day to say how much they had enjoyed the evening, And had they thanked him for a great evening. After all, the guy had arranged everything and had paid for it all too. The girls had taken everything on offer and then said good night.

Put yourself in their shoes. You have asked a girl out on a date and then gone out of your way to make it enjoyable and memorable, which it was, and you paid for everything. At the end of the evening the girl says thanks and good night. And then the next day, you hear nothing from her. You wait another day. Still nothing.

I suggested to these girls that they might have contacted the fellow first thing the following morning with a cheery hello, a huge thank you, and an invitation for a cup of coffee and a walk in the park.

They looked at me, thought about it for a moment, and then said, gosh you're right, why didn't we think of that?

Seize the moment, take a chance. You will be surprised at the result.

11. Eyes on him

Imagine this, you are out with a guy and you keep noticing that he is always looking around the room, checking out the action, checking out the other girls...think how that would make you feel.

Too many women do this all the time. Hey, I know everybody does it, but if you're going to do it, do you really want to get caught. There is no upside in this strategy. You might get away with it if you are out with a sardine, but you shouldn't be in that situation to begin with. Swimming with the sardines means you are a sardine too. And sardines don't eat tuna in my neighbourhood.

And if you have followed this guide so far and are enjoying a nice evening with your prospective tuna, why in the world would you want to jeopardize it all with an easily spotted glance around the room to see what else is swimming nearby. Crazy. Big downside risk, zero upside potential.

And yet, I see this happen all the time.

While the amateurs are blowing their hard fought for chances with their tuna; the clever girls are making their tuna the center of their universe. They keep their eyes on the prize.

I was lucky enough one day to have a hit on a tennis court with a well known professional player. Of course I wanted him to tell me that I had lots of talent, and that I just needed to adjust my grip a little or change the way I hit the ball a little and I would immediately be a better player. Instead he told me something completely different. He told me to watch the ball. Watch the ball? Are you kidding? Of course I watch the ball. Surely it would be impossible to hit the ball unless I was watching it, right? Wrong.

He told me that I was taking my eye off the ball just before I made contact. Hard to believe but true. He told me about an all time great called Ivan Lendl who used to hit a thousand backhands down the line in a practice session, and he never took his eye off the ball until it had left his racket. He didn't need to look at it after that because he had hit it so well that he knew exactly where it was going and where it would land.

Do the same thing.

Keep your eye on your target. And don't take it off. If he's a smart guy then he will be watching you too, and he won't take kindly to you checking out his competition under his very eyes. Very hard to get a tuna to fall in love with you with that strategy. So there is no reason to do it.

Unless you are absolutely sure that your tuna will not spot you checking out the other fish in the sea while you are with him, then don't do it.

It works both ways too. Keep your eye on him and see what he is seeing too.

And if he is always looking over your shoulder, then it is time to raise your game or reel in your line and move on. But chances are, if you are playing it right, then he'll only have eyes for you, and you'll know it too.

12. Mystery

It is often better to travel than to arrive, as the old saying goes.

Similarly, once your big tuna knows everything there is to know about you, he might not keep coming back for more.

There is a certain allure to anything mysterious, so work hard to develop it. Always keep something back. Do not be too free and easy with any kind of information about yourself. Feel free to allude to anything that you think might capture his imagination, but do not fill in the details too quickly. Keep him guessing. Wondering what's next.

It doesn't matter if your job is hum drum at the best of times. Don't let him know. There is also no reason to big it up. Just keep the information flow down to a trickle.

Imagination is a curious thing. If you have played your cards right so far, found a good fishing spot for a big tuna, got one on the end of your hook, and you're now starting to reel him in, the best way to keep his interest up and the suspense building is to be mysterious.

This doesn't mean being evasive. Well, not obviously so. But it is. And the less you say about yourself the more he will want to know. And if he is starting to fall for you he will be careful not to pry too aggressively into your business and background, at least not that you can see. Sure, he'll be on his computer trying to see what he can find out about you online, but that's it, and if he's doing that then you're winning the game anyway. So keep playing it that way.

Fun Girl was a minor celebrity. She worked as a columnist for a big gossip magazine and had quite a following, albeit for being a personality rather than for any great accomplishment that she'd actually achieved. When a new tuna presented itself, and he asked her if she was famous, she'd reply, "I'm known". Brilliant answer. Means whatever you want it to mean. Known by whom? Known by a thousand people, a million, or just a hundred? Known in your local village, or on the big screen? Known for what? Looks, dodgy dealings, player, what? An answer like that builds interest, builds suspense, and builds power.

Rock Chick is particularly good at playing this game, and she would downplay her family's accomplishments. The fact that both sides of her family had run governments in the Middle East and Asia was not something that she mentioned until the tuna was practically on the table and ready to be devoured.

As a further example, another ruthlessly successful player of this game, Mystery Lady, used another little trick. She did not come from an illustrious family nor was she a very big personality. But she was good at something that is of interest to most guys. Sex. And her game was to be very mysterious when it came to what she does, has done, where, with whom, while alone, at what time of the day, night, in which location, how often, how many ways, which positions, her fantasies, and what turns her on.

She had been seeing a guy for about eighteen months, on and off, and playing the field the whole time too. She had a feeling that the guy was onto her, and knew she had to up her game a little to entice him back to where she wanted him, which was under her control.

They were in bed, and enjoying a vigorous but standard session of missionary sex. He was thinking that this might be the last time, because he had grown weary of all her lies and all her other guys. So, he let a finger venture into a previously unexplored cavity of hers, located below the belt. He expected her to recoil in disgust. But, being clever, as Mystery Lady was, she let him do it. And instead of reacting with disgust, she started moaning with pleasure, as she had never done so (with him) before. In fact, she started screaming with ecstasy, so loudly, that he was worried that the neighbours might hear and complain. When it was all over, and they were lying next to each other quietly, he said "How come I have known you for all this time and yet I only find out now that you like that?" She replied that he had never asked, and that being English, she was not able to volunteer the information without being prompted. He thought about that for a minute and then said, "What else do you like to do in bed that I don't know about?" She replied, "Oh, there is lots, but I can't tell you everything in one go just like that."

This guy was astounded. You mean there is a lot more to know about this girl in terms of what she likes to do in bed, and he will never know if he chucks her?

Her little trick worked. He didn't chuck her.

If you think about it for a moment this is an extremely powerful weapon to have in your armoury...

Have a little think and see if there is something that you can develop a knack for being mysterious about, and then work it.

The golden rule though is to keep travelling, and not to arrive. Always keep something back. Or, at the very least, make sure that he thinks that he doesn't know everything there is to know about you.

A little mystery will keep him coming back for more, and more, and more.

And if he gets bold and puts you on the spot about something, just say with a smile, "that's for me to know and for you to find out".

13. Focus

Working on the basis that this is a business rather than a little game, it is worth remembering the importance of having focus at all times. And that focus point should be your tuna.

It is very important that you gather and collect as much information about this guy as you can. You need to know him inside out, what he likes and doesn't like. And that can only happen if you study him like a priest studies his bible. Of course you can not let him know that he is being watched with extreme purpose, but that is what you should be doing.

If you do this well then by the end you will have an encyclopaedic knowledge of your prey, and you should be able to predict his movements and actions with ease. This ability will enable you to anticipate problems, and to head them off before they have a chance to develop into something serious.

It will also mean that an alarm bell will go off if something out of the ordinary starts to happen. Something that might not work to your advantage. Similarly, if you know your target well, as a result of your sharp focus, it will give you room for manoeuvre.

As an example of this at its most basic level, your tuna's birthday should be engraved on the inside of your skull. And if you are running two or three tuna at the same time, then their birthdates should all be engraved inside your skull. Nothing shows interest as easily and effectively as a sweet birthday card and thoughtful message, delivered on time. And nothing shows a lack of real interest as obviously as forgetting about it entirely.

I have seen marriages seriously jeopardized by a spouse's neglect in observing their partner's birthday. Scarcely believable, but true. Conversely, I have seen women who are very good at playing this game make amends for some horrendous behaviour through the simple act of delivering an appropriate card at the right time.

So pay very careful attention to what your tuna says to you, and keep those facts safe. If you have a bad memory, then write it down. If he tells you that his mother was an orphan and that he has a dog called Ty, then write it down.

Look at how he dresses, what he drives, where he lives, where he works, what he likes to eat, which beer he drinks, football team he supports, games he plays, colours he likes, his style, where he goes on vacation, his age, his hair style, the shoes he wears, which brands he likes and doesn't like, his religion, political stance, and keep a mental note of all of it.

Every piece of information about him that you can gather will help you to develop your own behaviour in such a way so that it will be impossible for him not to fall in love with you.

Now what is the point of gathering all this information. The point is to use it and to make sure you use it well.

Rock Chick had noticed that despite the fact that her tuna was a highly paid professional, he didn't appear to care too much about his appearance. In fact, he only owned three pairs of trousers, and one pair was full of holes. Instead of deriding him for his obvious lack of fashion sense, she had a female friend of hers point out the fact that his trousers had holes but she added the remark that he must be from a very rich family to have the confidence to go about in that style. Of course, the guy was a little embarrassed that the holes were of any great importance, but then he was also a little flattered that they had been noticed and commented upon. Shortly thereafter, Rock Chick bought some new trousers for him which he tried on, she told him how great he looked, and he hardly took them off again until they were completely worn out.

In another instance, a tuna told Fun Girl that he had always wanted a tattoo. She said nothing at the time, but quietly filed it away for future use. Life went on, and one day she got a chance to get a free tattoo courtesy of a famous TV series documenting the profiles of people who get tattoos. She had one done, and also arranged for her tuna to get one too. Not only would it be free of charge, but it would be done by the same tattoo artist who did the famous tattoo on David Beckham, and it would be filmed for worldwide viewing.

He went ahead and got the tattoo, and is now very pleased every time someone he knows walks up to him and says, "hey, I think I saw you on the Discovery Channel last night, was that really you?"

Now I'm not saying that you need to be able to make arrangements like these to land your big tuna, but what you can and should be doing is remembering little things about him that he mentions, and then doing something with that information that shows that you care and that you are thinking about him.

A girl I know had a tuna who liked a certain type of cheesecake that they only sell in Harrods, an upmarket department store in the middle of London. When her target tuna went to New York for two weeks on business she had a cheesecake from Harrods delivered to him at his office. This went down very well.

Whether it is buying a new pair of trousers or a cheesecake for your target tuna, it is the focus that enables you to do the right thing to win his affections. The more you focus, the sooner you will have that tuna hooked, landed, gutted, and grilled.

14. Sexy Baby

If you aren't using sex to land your big tuna then you may as well go home and get used to a diet of sardines for dinner. Small ones.

Anyone who tells you anything to the contrary is smoking too much jaba or else he or she has a hidden agenda. What made Marilyn Monroe the undisputed sexual icon of the last century? Sex appeal. How come every man and virtually every woman, if she is being truthful, would like to sleep with Angelina Jolie? Sex appeal. How come everybody likes Jennifer Aniston but she can't seem to keep her man. Lack of sex appeal.

If you think that maybe you can rely on your charm, intelligence, and personality to land the big one, good luck. Why do things the hard way when it is unnecessary. And why let your competition have one over on you. You can enjoy your "pretty and nice" reputation or you can benefit from your "skanky and vice" rep. You choose.

If you don't believe me then take a trip to Pattaya, known as "Sin City" in Thailand. This city attracts millions of visitors from around the world every year, attracted by the tropical climate, the culture, delicious food, and the beautiful islands and beaches, all at very affordable third world prices. But go back a few years and you will learn that Pattaya's main attraction, before it cleaned up it's act and started attracting families and the like, was the women who made themselves available to single male tourists, starting with the American soldiers enjoying a little rest and recreation away from the battles being fought in the jungles just across the border in Vietnam.

If you walk around Pattaya after dark today, you will see countless numbers of bars full of women dressed up for a big night out. Funnily enough, you will also see men dressed up as women who look even better. These women have one purpose in mind, to attract the attention of men, and to make as much money out of them as is possible. And the first question they will ask that man is "how long you stay in Thailand?" Then they will say "you very sexy man". Then they will ask him to buy them a drink, and then another and another. The man will soon become inebriated, pay the establishment a "bar fine", a small fee to take her home with him, and then promptly pass out. The next day he will pay her a small fortune, in her terms, for a night he can not remember. She will look into his eyes, say sweet things, compliment him, and then attempt to get him to do it all over again the next evening. If she is really good then she will be playing several of these stupid men at the same time.

If she has enough time to get her hook into him, then he is done for. As soon as he returns home to his suburban life in Manchester he will be dreaming of the dark skinned tropical beauty he met on holiday, and chances are he will start sending her money on a monthly basis.

Don't believe me? Thailand receives millions of dollars of hard currency inflows every week from Western Europe. And all paid for by gullible sardines.

Well the same principles apply here. The main difference is that you are fishing for bigger prey. And that requires a little more subtlety in approach, but it's not a whole lot different. These Thai women can normally work their magic on Mr. Sardine in about three weeks. Catching a tuna takes a little longer, but still no more than 60 days.

If you are trying to do it without using every ounce of your particular brand of sex appeal then it is like running a marathon with a suitcase strapped to your back. Possible, but very hard work.

I have previously mentioned the ladies who know how to do it, the four ladies who are experts at fishing for tuna. I call them Fun Girl, Rock Chick, Mystery Lady, and Thai Dancer. They couldn't be more different from one another in looks, temperament, and bearing. But they all know the best fishing spots, use the best bait, and land the biggest tuna, and lots of them.

The one thing they all have in common is sex appeal. And boy do they know how to use it.

Conversely, I also know lots of very attractive women who struggle with their fishing lines. They spend a lot of time on their equipment but they just don't seem to get many bites. And when they do, somehow the fish always seems to get off the line.

These women have good looks, but not much in terms of sex appeal.

So you're probably wondering, does that mean I have to behave like a slut to catch a big tuna. No, but lots of men like that approach, even if they'll never admit it to your face or to their sisters. How you should behave will depend on how well you have studied your tuna, how well you have listened, and what you have managed to pick up about him, plus what your instinct is telling you about him.

Then, to quote J Pow, my favourite Cambodian philosopher, it is "up to you".

But just remember one thing before you decide. Brad left Jennifer for Angelina, and it wasn't for her cooking...

15. Speculate to Accumulate

Pay your way. Shock horror. That's correct. I'm suggesting that the way to land the Big Tuna is to pay your way. Change that. It is not a suggestion. It is a command. Do not under any circumstances allow him to pay. Make sure that you have cash and a credit card at all times. And make sure that you use them both.

So you are meeting him at a bar for drinks and then you're going for dinner to a nice restaurant around the corner. He's there when you arrive and has already bought a bottle of champagne or pinot noir. So he's beaten you to it. This means that dinner is on you. But wait a second, you're saying, he buys drinks and I buy dinner? But that's going to cost me way more than drinks cost him. Correct. Do it. Pay. If necessary, excuse yourself before you order coffee and give the waiter your credit card and tell him that he is to charge dinner to your card, no matter what the Big Tuna says or does. Say it, and mean it. When it comes time to sign the receipt or punch in your PIN number into the machine, do it without a thought or a care. And then look at him, smile, and thank him for a wonderful evening.

This simple act will make the strongest impression possible for a woman to make. It flies in the face of societal norms; it will confuse and bewilder him, and once it has sunk in, will impress the pants off him to an unimaginable degree. It will mark you out from the rest, put you into a league all of your own, and establish you in his mind as that rarest of animals, a woman who contributes rather than a woman who just takes.

Think about the message it sends. It says that you are fair. It says that you aren't taking advantage of him. It says that you aren't a user. It says that you value him and his company. It says that you aren't a whore. It says that you don't see him as a meal ticket. It says that you don't need him to provide. It says that you are successful. It says that you are different from all the rest, and it gives you an edge.

Let's look at the impact it makes on him. He goes away thinking that he can't buy you. That you aren't for sale. That you have self respect as well as respect for him. And it will make him want you. Not for a lust filled night of fun. Not for a quick fling. He'll be so impressed that he'll automatically start thinking that he's found The One, his soul mate, the woman to have children with and to grow old with. Here's a girl unlike all the rest. Wow. A keeper. And the part of the brain that produces the hormone that makes men fall stupidly in love will start pumping massive amounts of that love drug into his bloodstream, and he'll be in love in no time.

You don't believe me. Sounds far fetched. You mean all I have to do is buy dinner and he'll fall in love with me, father my children, buy me a large German four wheel drive SUV, a big house, and pay for everything for the rest of my life? Yup. Why is that? Because you are different from the rest. Of course you'll have to follow all the other rules outlined here as well, but this is an important piece of the puzzle. Skip the Pay your Way rule, and the cost will be much higher.

The funny thing about paying your way, being generous, getting your money out and using it, is that the more you spend on him, the more he'll end up spending on you. Spend $5 today; get back $50 in future. You should regard such expenditure as an investment. Kind of like playing the stock market. Except that the returns will be a lot better. And you will not lose.

Remember to spend the money, even if you don't have a lot to spare. If the Big Tuna has any brains he'll have already worked out your likely income level from your house and car and the clothes you wear. And if he suspects that your income is at a level which makes the bill for dinner a little painful, then his admiration for you can only increase. He'll be sure that you must really like him. And this is a good thing for him to think.

I've already said that this strategy works because it separates you from the competition. He'll look at you and think he's hit the jackpot and found a partner for life. But it doesn't end there. The next time he's talking to his friends down at the golf club or over beers after work and your name comes up he'll take great delight in proudly telling them that you bought him dinner. Why. Because this action tells the guys that their friend and your tuna must be pretty special. After all, can anyone else at the table tell a similar story? Almost certainly not. The word will go out that this new girl on the scene, i.e. you, is pretty special. And that she likes the Big Tuna a lot. The Big Tuna will swell with pride. The other guys will envy and admire him. And they will all want to meet you.

Next time the Big Tuna is in the mall or walking past a jewellery shop he might just be tempted to stop in and pick out a fancy trinket or two for presentation at the next dinner, paid for, of course, by him.

Whatever you spend on him will be returned ten, twenty, or even a thousand times over. And it will help ensure that you get the hook in deep into the Big Tuna. Very deep. Does that sound like it might be worth the investment of the price of dinner?

Women often make the mistake of thinking that since it is customary for the guy to pay, that he wants to pay, and feels like a man when he does so. Wrong. Sure, there are plenty of idiots who feel that way. But they are also the types who tend to buy red sports cars, and wear baseball caps backwards well into middle age. We are not talking here about a species of Big Tuna. Maybe a decent tasting bottom fish, but not a King of the Sea like a tuna. If you're happy with a flounder, or a Dover sole, then let the sucker pay all the way, but don't complain later that you're living down on the seabed instead of up near the surface where the sun shines brightly.

There are lots of examples of women who do well enough without ever reaching into their purse to pay their way. The problem for them is that it only gets them so far, and often the man has them clocked anyway, and as soon as their trophy looks fade, or a newer model comes along, the guy switches fast. Play the game my way and you've got the guy for as long as you want him.

It is important not to be too obvious about your strategy here. If the guy thinks you're making the mental calculation of own money expended versus his money received he'll run. Nobody, not even a dumb sucker, likes to be played. It is humiliating. So get it right. I've seen women proffer their credit card, as if they are going to pay, but with the knowledge that the offer will be refused. Be careful. The guy could easily test the water and call your bluff and allow you to pay. So don't offer to pay if you can't do so. Similarly, always have some cash on you. I was in a cab going up Park Lane with a woman one afternoon. We'd had lunch and I had paid. We were going to a gallery exhibition in Mayfair, organized by me. When I realized I was a little short of cash for the cab fair and asked her for £10 to make up the fare, she looked in her purse but didn't have the required £10. Nor did she have £5. Another time, and at the end of another date with a different woman, I dropped her off at the train station to find her way home. I hadn't been too impressed by her and had no desire to see her again. She was surprised that she wasn't coming back with me, and as we found out, unprepared and unable to make her way home because she didn't have a penny on her. Of course I marked them both down sharply, but on later reflection had to give myself a hard time too, because it was obvious that both women had been playing me, taking me, and using me for what they could get. Not a nice feeling. I learned something from the experiences, but I suspect that both women didn't, and they're probably both still taking guys for a ride, but ending up with not a lot to show for it when all is said and done.

Another woman was in the early stages of a romance with a very successful man when he called her one day and said he was in a bit of a financial jam and needed to borrow some money fast. She lent him £10,000. It was a trifle to him, but her entire life savings. She got her money back two weeks later. He fell in love with her. When they got married later, she paid for the wedding celebrations. He was having liquidity problems again. Fifteen years later and they have four children, a private plane, several multi-million dollar properties, and a five star life style. Her husband, who had been used to dating lots of very attractive women before he met his wife, told me that the short term loan had distinguished the woman he ended up marrying from all the rest of the girls he had been seeing. He was massively impressed. And she landed the Big Tuna as a result.

There is no reason to be silly with this strategy. I'm not telling you to pay for everything, or to go overboard with the expenditure because you'll make back ten or twenty times the amount you spend. The whole idea is give you an edge over the competition. To make you stand out from the crowd. And money evokes powerful feelings in most people, at the conscious and the sub-conscious level. A guy may want to play the big spender because he wants to make an impression, but that doesn't mean he wants to be ripped off or taken for granted, or played for a fool. And by showing that you can and do pay occasionally, you're giving him a subtle reassurance that you're as into him as he is to you, even if you aren't. If it isn't true, it is still reassuring. And by reassuring him that you're different from the rest, you're getting the hook in a little deeper. One day you will want that hook in as deep as it goes, but more on that a little later.

16. A Dream Come True

Beauty is in the eye of the beholder. We all know that. But I am continually surprised by the obvious differences in taste that exist between men when it comes to comparing women according to their looks.

Some guys like skinny girls, some guys like their women to have plenty of "back". Then there's the whole big boob conundrum. So many women go out and get the boob job despite their husband or boyfriend begging them not to do it.

But none of it really matters at all. And here's the rub. A guy may tell you that he likes skinny blondes, and he may even believe it himself. And then an opportunity will arise with a fuller figured brunette, and as long as she says and does the right things at the right time, then he'll be smitten. Look around and think about the people you know. I bet you know of cases where a friend finishes a long relationship with one type, and then has the next relationship with someone who couldn't be more different from the last one. Different in terms of looks, and different in terms of personality, interests, fashion sense, humour, music, taste in food, drink, entertainment, I could go on.

So how is that, you're wondering. The answer is that we're all much more flexible in terms of what we actually find attractive than we think. Which means that we're much more open minded about who we fall in love with than you could ever imagine. I have been in love as an adult four times. The women could not have been more different from each other in the looks department. But at the time, I found each of them incredibly attractive. Now while it is true that they were very different from each other, the one thing that they all shared was an interest in looking good. And despite not all being raving beauties, they all looked like my dream come true, at the time. I couldn't believe my luck. A guy like me with a girl like that. Wow.

So I am constantly surprised again when I go out for an evening and see women who clearly haven't made an effort. Or they haven't looked in the mirror to determine if their ensemble actually works, or not. Leggings are incredibly revealing. And sure, I understand that they are incredibly comfortable and all that. But look girls, save the comfort option for your pyjama party at home with your best girlfriend. When you go out for some tuna fishing, if uncomfortable looks better and it gets a nibble from a Big Tuna then you're going uncomfortable.

Hair up. You can not be serious.

It's simple. You never know who you're going to meet. And you don't know when the Big Tuna is going to glide into view. So you've gone out for a drink with your girlfriend, just the two of you, and you're at the bar ordering drinks and along comes the big one. He looks great. You're so close that you can smell his deodorant. But you're a few pounds overweight because you've had a Chardonnay heavy summer, and you've come out in your comfy leggings, and because of all this you haven't bothered to do your hair, so it's all tied up in a mess. Hardly compelling. Because of all this you're not flying at your natural confidence level, and it takes you a while to think of something to say or do to start something with him, and because of the delay and the way you look, he's gone, and the moment has passed. You blew it.

If only you had been in the habit of always looking your best. And even if you are a little heavier than your optimum fighting weight, you're wearing something that disguises the weight, rather than leggings which accentuate it. You took some time to do something, anything, with your hair, rather than tie it back up. And if you had done that, the conversation might have flowed when the chance arose, and you'd be going home at the end of the evening hopeful that there would be another chance with the Big Tuna when you meet for a drink later in the week, because you've exchanged numbers after a quick chat.

These things are fragile. They either happen easily or it all becomes difficult and just doesn't flow. You know what I'm talking about. And it is an animal thing. You feel good about the way you look, opportunities arise because of the vibe you're giving off, and hey ho the big fish come to you. You're not looking your best, your vibe is off, and the fish back away, looking for tastier morsels elsewhere. The difference is how you look and how it makes you feel as a result. And it doesn't take a lot to get the look right. A little effort and a little discipline. But the results from doing it right versus wrong are huge. Life changing.

In an earlier chapter I mentioned somebody whom I know, and called her Fun Girl. This woman never steps out of the house without looking like a million dollars. Admittedly she is a good looking woman to begin with. However, she's had a very serious illness, she's carrying a few extra pounds, and she doesn't have a lot of money for expensive clothes or beauty treatments. Despite all this, she always looks as if she's about to go onto a film set, her hair is done, her clothes are stylish and very well put together, her nails are always done, and she'll set it all off with one or two pieces of distinctive but inexpensive jewellery. Whether she walks into a grubby pub in Camden or into an exclusive west end restaurant, she always means business and she looks her best. And when an opportunity arises and she gets a chance to exchange a few words with a Big Tuna, the poor guy hardly stands a chance. As a result, she's lived with a famous rock star for years, before dumping him and moving onto a TV star, and she's had all numbers of famous and successful men standing outside her flat late at night begging for her to let them in so that they can come upstairs for a chat. Remember that this is a woman without a single qualification to her name, she's never had a proper job, she has no money, doesn't own a home, and can't have children. And yet she has men of all ages begging her for a chance to be a part of her life.

If anyone tells you that you need a lot of money or expensive clothes or anything other than a smile, a good personality, a zest for life, and a good attitude to catch a Big Tuna then they should meet this woman. Men take her on holiday and pay for everything. She doesn't have a bean but she'll always buy the first drink. And whatever she has she gives away. And she always looks good.

You do the same, and it will pay off big time.

17. Listen Up

Listen to him. Don't just pay attention. Really listen.

Just imagine that you have an exam in two months time and you
have to learn everything you can about a certain subject before
then. If you pass the exam then it could change your life in a big
way. If you fail then you stay right where you are.

So the question is how much you want things to change. Do you
want to get an A+, or are you happy with a D.

If you decide to go for gold, then it really is just a matter of
application.

My grandfather told me about the world's best Checkers player.
Remember that game from when you were a kid. It was fun, but
it got kind of boring after a while, especially if something really
fun came up. But have you ever seen a really good player play
the game? Wow. They literally destroy their opponent, moving
backwards and forwards taking the other guy's pieces with ease.

The Checkers Champ was good because he applied himself. He
studied the game, and that's all he did. And that was why nobody
could beat him.

If you study the behaviour of your tuna then you will be equally successful on your various fishing trips. And listening well is the first step to becoming an expert on your tuna.

Listen to everything he says. Absorb it. And remember it too. In order to do this, it will require that you refrain from talking about yourself. That is difficult for a lot of people, but it is essential to know when to talk and when to listen.

Many friends of mine will go on a date and then report back. Often I hear about how good looking their date was, what she was wearing, the colour of her hair, her height. Generally speaking men like to boast to other men about how attractive their dates are, even if it is not true. It's a male ego thing, I guess. I then ask them how it went and ask them if they are going to see the girl again. Then I get a long pause, followed by a tilt of the head, and then an "I'm not sure".

So you're wondering, if she was so attractive, how come he isn't all over her with dinner reservations, invitations to the movies, and tickets to see the ballet.

Too often, it seems that the date consisted of the girl talking incessantly about herself. Her job, her kids, her ex-husband or ex-boyfriend, her problems at work, problems with certain family members, her divorce, money troubles, you get the picture. The polite guy sat there and listened, and when it was all done he got to pay the bill. More often than not, apparently, the date neither offered to pay her share, nor even had the courtesy to say thank you.

One poor guy I know took a girl to see an early movie, which he paid for, and then for dinner at an expensive Italian restaurant off the Kings Road in London. When it came to choosing the wine, they ordered white in spite of the fact that the guy didn't really like white wine very much, but the girl did. Over a three course dinner, the girl talked non-stop about her family and her job. She also explained that she was currently on a "man ban" because of a broken relationship. At no point did she ask her big tuna prospect anything about him. She just talked and talked and talked, about herself. She even had the audacity to tell him that when they had first met, that she "wasn't really into it".

When the bill came, he paid. No offer from her and no contribution.

When they left the restaurant and were walking up the road towards the car, she said, "oh no, I was going to pay the tip".

Apparently the girl had a great night. She went home and told her friends the next day that this really good looking, wealthy, single guy took her out for a great dinner at a great restaurant where she ordered everything she wanted, and the guy was great too because he was very attentive, and listened to everything she said, and he paid for everything too.

Then she waited for the next invitation. And waited. And waited. After about a month of waiting she couldn't stand it any longer. After all, she was a 40 year old lady with a great sense of humour, the body of a woman ten years younger, very pretty, and yet he hadn't been in touch. Had he lost her number, perhaps? Maybe he was sick, or travelling on business, or with his family or daughter. She had to know.

So she contacted him by text. And asked, "why didn't you call?"

The guy got the text and thought, revenge really is a dish best served cold. He was tempted to tell her that the reason is that he didn't really relish the prospect of another evening that would cost him £250 for the pleasure of drinking wine he didn't really like, with a woman who didn't care what he liked, or listening to someone talk about themselves and their problems for the best part of three hours.

He thought about it some more, and then texted back, "I was waiting for you to call me."

The truth was that he found her very attractive. She was funny, and witty, and very pretty. But a night out with her was all about her. He was the walking wallet.

After three dates with this woman, he wasn't really sure if she even knew his full name. She hadn't asked him anything about himself, except where he lived, what he did for a living, and how tall he was.

With a strategy like that she will not get far in the Big Tuna fishing competition.

The man was ripe for the picking. He had been out of a relationship that had gone sour for about six months, the wounds had healed, and he was ready and interested in starting afresh. Along comes this very pretty girl, so he gives it a whirl, and then is disappointed to meet yet another woman who only talks about herself.

If you want your date to have a better result, then ask him about himself.

And then let him talk.

Most people like talking about themselves if they think they have an interested audience. So you can turn this to your advantage. Ask him what kind of movies he likes to go and see. Ask him if he likes red wine or white. Ask him if he prefers Italian or Thai food. Ask him about his job, his friends, his family, his dreams, his intentions, his situation, his vacations, his life.

Chances are he will talk and talk and talk, and he will love you for listening.

18. Quick off the mark

Time is precious, and time is money.

You simply can not afford to waste time with the wrong guys.

Don't get me wrong, some times the wrong guys are the most fun. But you are here to land the big tuna, so you are doing the fishing. Be careful that you don't get caught on someone else's hook.

Remember that there are men out there who are playing a similar game to you. They are not necessarily looking for someone to provide for them, but they like women, especially pretty ones. And they like sex, and are often very good at it, and these are the guys to avoid.

They come in several different guises. But they belong to a species called Mirage Men. They look good but aren't when you get up close.

The crude variety of Mirage Man drives a flashy car, wears designer clothes, has good hair, knows all the right places and takes all the right drugs. But the car is probably financed, his job and true earning prospects are not stellar, he spends too much time looking in the mirror, his friends are drug dealers and he owes them money. All flash, not much cash.

The more sophisticated Mirage Man has a much better act. He alludes to his real estate holdings, his various businesses, and his stock market portfolio. He is a more conservative dresser, and drives a nice car, but nothing too fancy. The problem with this type is that the houses will be heavily mortgaged, the businesses will be pledged to the bank, and both will be used to finance his stock market dealings, which may not be going too well. But he won't tell you about that.

With the flashy guy, there isn't a lot of cash left to provide for you, after he has bought all his hair products and designer clothes. With the conservative fellow, anything that he really has left, after all the loans have been paid back, will probably go to his ex-wife in alimony.

Remember that Donald Trump was a self-confessed negative billionaire at the time when people thought he was loaded. Alan Bond, the Australian tycoon who won the America's Cup made a habit of throwing the biggest parties when he was struggling financially the most.

So these are examples of what's out there, and what can trip you up. There are lots of fish that look like a big tuna, but they aren't the real deal, and you need to avoid at all costs. They will suck you in with a good game, and you will waste a lot of time with them, and may even fall in love, they are that good. So beware.

You need to figure out exactly what you are dealing with, and fast. It is easy to check up on people these days. As long as you know a person's name, you can even check out his credit score for a small fee.

If the guy says he went to a top university, find out if it is true. Google his name and see what comes up. Ask his friends about him, how long they have known him, is he a good guy, what happened with his previous relationships, and is he good at his job. If possible, find out the name of his ex, and see if it is possible to contact her through a mutual acquaintance. Beyond that, it comes down to experience and instinct. If your instinct is not good about people, ask a friend who is good to take a look and tell you what he or she thinks.

I know a woman who met a good looking guy, on the face of it extremely successful. He was a doctor, and had been one of the early pioneers of the laser surgery industry. He had a successful surgery business, three huge houses in beautiful locations, and was retired. His story was that he was looking to start a new business in the stem cell field, and he claimed that he could cure any disease with his new stem cell technology. He wasn't doing it for the money, because he already had plenty. He was doing it for the benefit of mankind.

It was a good story. Very plausible, and he was very credible.

So she got involved with him. Believed everything he said. She did think it was a little strange that he was looking through her phone while she was asleep at night. And that he used to spend a lot of time in her office, no doubt looking through her personal papers. She was a wealthy woman.

One weekend I heard that she had gone skiing for the weekend, at his invitation. She had flown two thousand miles to stay with him at his trophy home in Aspen. I got a call from her on Saturday afternoon. She told me that she was skiing for the day, alone. That her boyfriend had left early on Saturday morning to fly to California for a meeting. And that she was calling me on her cell phone, despite the fact that I was in Italy, because his home phones didn't work. And neither did his computer.

It didn't add up.

She found out later that he had gone to Los Angeles to attend a dinner. He couldn't invite her because he only had one ticket. As my Grandmother would say, a likely story.

She carried on with him for far too long, wasted too much time.

It turned out that the guy had gone bankrupt ten years earlier. A doctor friend brought him in to his business and taught him everything there was to know about spine surgery with lasers. And the Mirage Man returned the favour by leaving and setting up a business in competition, which did very well.

Unfortunately for him, he then used his business to borrow ten million dollars to buy a house. This was at the top of the property boom. When the bubble burst, the house was only worth five million. He was cheating on his wife, for the umpteenth time, so she kicked him out. Then he performed back surgery on a famous athlete. It was not successful and the athlete sued him, and it got into the papers and onto the internet. The bad publicity hit his business hard.

At the time that he met this friend of mine, he was a negative millionaire with a washed up career. His wife was soon to be awarded millions in her divorce settlement, the big house would be hers too, and the bank would end up taking the business which had been pledged as collateral against the mortgage on the house. His professional reputation was in tatters. The stem cell thing was a scam. He was looking to hoodwink gullible investors into giving him millions in return for a stake in the new business. And if anybody asked him why he didn't invest in the new business himself, he'd say that he was getting divorced and couldn't do it. If a serious investor took a look and started asking the right questions, he walked away.

When this friend of mine finally discovered the truth, she was shocked.

The fool had come over to the woman's house one day and had spent some time on her computer, working, he said. Once he had left, she went to do some work on her computer and realized that her boyfriend, not being too good with technology, had mistakenly minimized windows instead of hitting the x button and closing them. So all she had to do was click on each window to see exactly what he had been up to while she had been baking cookies for her kids.

The truth was shocking.

He was on a dating website for supposed millionaires.

He was on a website for "Sugardaddys", which introduces older rich guys to young models and students in need of financial assistance.

And he had another girlfriend. She was a film maker, and she was seeking film finance. He had promised a lot but delivered nothing. The emails between them showed that she was getting tired of his excuses and offers to introduce her to people who would finance her film, but only if she promised to give him the starring role in the movie.

The simple truth was that he was worse than broke, despite the big properties, the Hummers, all the boys' toys, and the businesses.

He was trying to scam my friend for money, or possibly, steal it. And he was trying to scam his other girlfriend into making him a movie star.

So do your homework before you decide to invest too much time and effort into a prospective big tuna. Make sure that he is what he says he is. And remember, if it looks too good to be true, then it is probably exactly that.

Figure out what you are really dealing with, and do it fast. And if things don't stack up, then cut your losses while they are still small.

There are plenty of big tuna in the sea.

19. Remember

Think about this for a moment. Let's say you meet somebody new and you get along well. You have a long conversation, and as sometimes happens when it feels good right from the start; you open up a little more than usual and tell this person a lot about yourself. The conversation just flows, and it is easy to talk. And the other person is listening but not saying a lot.

The conversation draws to a close because one or both of you have to go. You exchange numbers and arrange to meet again.

Later on that day, you start to wonder if you have said too much, told this person whom you don't really know just a little bit too much about yourself. You feel a little embarrassed. After all, this is a complete stranger to you, and yet you have revealed some pretty intimate details about yourself. But then you think about it some more and decide that your impression of this other person was really good, so why not. What do you have to lose?

Anyway, some time later you meet this other person again, and you start off as before. You open up and reveal some more private information about yourself. After all, you have already decided that there is no harm in doing so, and so you talk freely as before.

The conversation, which is a little lop-sided, because you are doing most of it, swings around and back to something that you said in the first meeting. At this point you realize that your new friend has forgotten something that you had said in the earlier chat. And it isn't something inconsequential, it is something really quite personal, and not something you have told a lot of people before about yourself.

A little alarm bell goes off inside. You suddenly wonder who this person is, what you have said that maybe you shouldn't have said, and get a little fearful about how information about yourself that this person might remember might be used against you in some way.

Not a nice feeling.

Now, imagine exactly the opposite outcome. Imagine that your new friend has remembered everything you told them about yourself. And instead of it raising the hairs on the back of your neck, you are really quite flattered. Flattered because here it looks as if this new friend of yours has not only listened, but listened with interest, and has remembered it too.

If you can remember what your tuna tells you then you are half way home to getting that fish on dry land and ready for the grill.

People can feign interest and pretend to listen. In fact, some people are really good. But remembering what you have been told is a different thing entirely.

And the effect that it can have on the speaker is significant. The speaker will like you for listening and will love you for remembering.

Really listening to what someone has to say, remembering it, and then replaying it back to that person at a later date is a skill well worth developing when it comes to tuna fishing.

It raises the level of intimacy better than anything, even sex.
And intimacy is the name of the game. You want your tuna to be more intimate with you than anyone he has ever known, in the romantic sense.

Despite rumours to the contrary, largely inspired by stereotypes put out by the media, men are more romantic than women. They don't want to admit it, because it isn't considered to be a very manly thing to be, but men want to be in love, they want to romance a woman, and they do.

Too many single women whom I know do exactly the opposite. They may talk the talk and appear to be very romantic, and they might even believe it. But when you look at their behaviour, they are not romantic at all. They love to be on the receiving end, but do nothing to develop or nurture it, and nothing to sustain it. There seems to be a belief, misguided at best, that it is the man's job to be romantic, to do all the wooing and courting, to buy the flowers, book the nice hotel, the fancy candle lit restaurant for dinner. The only thing the woman has to do is to make herself look pretty, turn up on time, and take what's offered.

That all seems very romantic for the woman, but how about the man. He's the one who has organized everything, after he has figured out what to do, where to go, and paid for it all. That's a lot of work. And a lot of thought and consideration. And what he does will say a lot about himself, it will reveal his notions of what romance should look like, and how it should be expressed. So for the guy there is a lot of pressure to get it right. It's all good as long as it is appreciated, but if he feels like he is being taken for granted, then there is scope for problems.

Now imagine the impact on the man if the lady does the thinking, the organizing, and shock horror, actually pays for the romantic evening instead. On top of that she listens attentively, and cleverly lets him know that she remembers everything he has ever said about himself to her that is deeply personal in nature.

Wow. What an impact that would make. And then imagine that the lady does it more than once.

Suddenly, from being lost somewhere in the pack of women that this big tuna is swimming around, you suddenly burst out and are swimming free of them all, and you will find him swimming alongside you, closely.

The funny thing is that you don't have to do a lot. Most single women make no effort at all. In fact they almost seem to go out of their way to wear a look and adopt a demeanour which says to any men in their vicinity that they are not interested in anybody at all. That they don't want to meet anybody, and that anybody they might meet is so far beneath their level that they wouldn't even give them a second of their time.

And that is one of the reasons why there are so many single women sitting at home after work tapping away on their computer while logged onto catch.com, all describing themselves and what they are looking for in the same bland way, and with the same results.

If you want romance, and if you want a romantic man, then the best way to get one is to start being romantic yourself.

And the most romantic thing a woman can do is to show that she is interested and that she cares. Not just on Valentine's, but all the time. Make the effort to listen to what the guy says, find out what turns him off and on, remember it, and then plan an hour, a day, an evening, or a week, that shows that you listened to what he said, and that you remembered, and then did something nice for him armed with that information.

If you can do that, then you can have anyone you want.

If it sounds like hard work then think again.

It can be something as simple as hearing from your tuna that he likes you to dress a certain way. He loves you in that pencil skirt with the starched white shirt. Or it could be a certain pair of jeans. If that's what he likes, then wear it. Maybe he is fascinated by Monster trucks, but has never been to see a real show. Buy some tickets. You may hate it, but that makes the impression on him even greater. Maybe he likes superfast powerboats. Organize and pay for a ride one sunny afternoon. It might be two hours of pain for you, but he'll remember it forever, and he'll remember who fixed it for him.

Let's go back to the example of Pattaya in Thailand, where the women are experts at treating their men well. Something really rather surprising happens there between the Thai women and the "Falang" men. Falang is the word in Thai for a western person.

A Falang man and a Thai woman hook up. Once she has her target, the Thai woman doesn't lack focus. Anywhere the Falang man goes, she goes. Anything he wants to do, she does. Any time, any day, any place. There is nothing she won't do to land her tuna.

Remember her game. She is looking for providers. Ideally she wants seven or eight Falang men to fall in love with her, to go back home to Western Europe, and to send her a thousand Euros every month. And it happens. To the untrained eye, it is easy to assume that the bait that she uses is sex. But the fact is that she is using romance to achieve her goal. Remember that after the Falang man goes back home that he is unlikely to see her again until the next 7,000 mile trip occurs and that might be six or more months away. However, he'll be paying her every month that he is away back in Europe, despite not getting any sex from her. It is romance, not sex that keeps the allure and the money flow going.

Believe it or not, but once a Thai lady in Pattaya has established a rapport with a Falang, she will be happy to go to a Go Go bar full of other Thai dancers, and sit quietly beside him while he gawks at the dancers in their limited attire. And he will love her for it. He'll tell his friends that he has found the most amazing woman. That he doesn't have to pretend with her, that he can relax and be himself, do the things he likes to do without fear of critical reproach.

Of course, the Thai lady is no different from you. But she is playing the game, and she is playing it well. Instead of sitting back and waiting to be entertained at somebody else's expense, as too many single women mistakenly do, she is making sure that he is having the best time of his life, and all because of her.

A beautiful Thai lady told me that she had spent two weeks with a Frenchman, and that towards the end of the two weeks the man had told her that he was going out that evening with some friends to watch some Thai boxing. Clearly, he thought that she would have no interest in joining them for some ringside entertainment. Of course, she had no interest in the boxing, but she had significant interest in keeping tabs on him. After all, she had invested two weeks time and effort in this guy, had made him feel like a king, and she wasn't going to run the risk after all that expenditure of effort that he was going to go out on the town without him and get waylaid by one of her competitors.

She demanded to go with him. He refused. After all, he thought, she was just a poor, uneducated girl from the countryside, and he was a debonair, sophisticate from Paris, with a fine family background and the world at his feet. He could go to the boxing without her if he wished and she could stay at home and watch a movie. So he went out.

But she didn't stay home and watch a movie. She hopped on a little baht taxi, one of those funny little pick-up trucks that they convert into taxis, where the passengers sit on benches at the back, and she cruised into town. She walked along Walking Street to Lucifer's, a bar popular with singles, and she saw him there. Not at the boxing, as he had said. But chatting to another girl. She made sure that he saw her, and then she grabbed another man and started chatting and dancing with him. Then she went back to their hotel, packed her belongings, and left.

He called and called. He sent texts. Many. And when he got back to Paris he continued to call and text. But all to no avail. She may have been a poor, uneducated girl, but she was no fool. And she knew that she could catch plenty more men like him, or even better. And so she did.

That girl now owns a farm with surrounding lands, and she has financed several businesses for her Thai friends and family, all of it funded by the men who fell for her, not because she was sexy, for she was, but because she was romantic too. She listened, and she remembered, and then she played it back. And when her various boyfriends from Australia, Norway, and America, went home, they thought about her and the way she had made them feel on their two or three week holiday with her.

Anybody can provide sex. Not everybody can be romantic. And the key to being romantic is to listen well, remember what makes a guy happy, and then provide it.

It isn't hard, and yet too many women today think that it is all about them, and that the way to get what they want is to wait for the perfect guy to come along and deliver. That might happen if you are a Victoria's Secret model and the guy is a brain dead emotional juvenile in love with the fantasy of going out with a Barbie doll rather than a real person, but if that isn't you then a new game is in order if you want to achieve your goals.

Be romantic and you will receive more romance than you can imagine. And start the process by listening, and listening well, and remembering.

20. Fast Sex

Men are dirty bastards. And I mean that in the nicest possible sense.

Men are also pretty simple. They like what they like, and as long as they get it they are for the most part happy.

And one of the things that men like is sex.

So give it to him. If you don't somebody else will. It is that simple. I'm not saying that you have to enjoy it, because that is not the point. If you want enjoyable sex then get that some place else if he isn't rocking your boat. Remember that this is business. You are after a big tuna to provide. If you are dreaming of meeting Mr. Perfect, the great looking, tall, sexy, rich dude who sweeps you off your feet and falls madly in love with you, then dream on. Chances are that he exists somewhere on this earth but I have met a lot of guys and I don't know anybody who fits that bill.

Which means a little compromise is in order. Consider also for a moment, if Mr. Perfect did come walking down the street and bumped into you, would he find you his female equivalent, or would he keep walking, thinking that there might be someone better, Miss Perfect, just around the corner.

Anyway, back to the task at hand. You've met a big tuna, you've been out with him a couple of times, so what happens next. From a guy's perspective, he has been wondering what you are like in bed from minute number one. If you've had two dates, and you're getting ready for number three, he's now thinking that if you like him and fancy him then tonight is the night.

He'll make sure his place is nice and tidy, there is a bottle of white wine in the refrigerator, and that the toilet seat is in the down position, ahead of his hoped for night of passion with you.

So do it.

Enjoy your dinner, and then go home with him. If you don't then you can kiss this one good bye. In fact there is an argument that says you have already left it too late, that if you want him to think that you fancy the pants off him, that he is irresistible to you, then you should have gone for it on the first night, and you should have asked him back to your place, and given him a night to remember.

You want him to go to work the next day feeling like King Stud. The other girls he has known probably kept him waiting. They liked his fancy car and career prospects and the lifestyle, but his man boobs were not a real turn-on, and his receding hairline was already in full retreat and yet he was only twenty eight.

So most girls took their time.

If you don't take your time then he's all yours. What's the real difference anyway. First date third date. So what. Fact is that I know lots of married couples who had sex on their first date. They don't like to admit it, but it's the truth. And it works.

If you don't then someone else will and what's the point of that. It means back to the drawing board all over again.

So have sex and make sure it is good. As I said before, men are dirty bastards. Sure, they may come across as all polished and civilized on the outside, but in bed it's different. As the old saying goes, a man wants a whore in his bed. And if he doesn't find one in your bed then he'll keep looking.

Be brave and be dirty. I'll guarantee the results.

I just mentioned that men are dirty bastards. So are women. Go on, admit it. Every woman I know, including my mother, has read 50 Shades of Grey. An ex-girlfriend of mine has read the trilogy. This was quite a shock because she was about as frigid as they came when she was going out with me. Or so I thought. Clearly there was more to her than meets the eye, and since she told a mutual friend of ours that her new boyfriend "is a very good lover", the fault was clearly with me. But I was younger back then, and hadn't realized yet that women are more complex that they might initially appear to be, at least on the surface.

So if you are honest with yourself and think back into the darkest recesses of your mind, the part where your sexual fantasies are stored, and dig up the sickest, most depraved and exciting fantasy that you have hidden back there, to be used only in your most private moments, then just imagine that tuna boy has the same. No, not the same fantasy, but his own private store of fantasies locked away in his wank bank.

Just like you, these are the fantasies that he is most ashamed of, the ones that make him squirm with embarrassment at the thought that anybody might know or find out. But they are also the thoughts that turn him on the most, and the fantasies that he would most like to turn into reality. His problem is that the women he meets are unlikely to be willing participants in one of his fantasies, or so he fears. And because he is scared to take the chance and ask his new girl whether she is fine with it or not, he never finds out. Why is this? It's because most people are too worried about being branded a pervert to take the risk and try something that they've always wanted to do but didn't for this very reason.

So tuna boy is caught in a Catch-22 situation.

If he fancies you, then the thing that would do it for him more than anything else would be to have you act as a willing participant in one of his 50 Shades'eque sexual dramas. And because he has played this fantasy in his mind at least fifty times before, he knows the story better than Quentin Tarantino knows his scenes in Pulp Fiction.

However, because he thinks you are a "nice girl", he thinks you'll make a face and say, "no way, I'm not doing that, it's not nice".

And so he doesn't ask.

And as a result, he'll take you out to dinner, and then have nice middle class sex with you afterwards, and there will be a weakness in your relationship. Something like the San Andreas Fault line in California. Remember that old Superman movie where Gene Hackman played the part of Lex Luther and he hatched a plan to cause an earthquake along the San Andreas Fault line which would cause the Californian coast line to fall into the water?

Well, the fact that you are not having the kind of dirty sex that he wants is going to be the fault line in your relationship. He'll play the part of the nice boyfriend, meet your parents, buy you nice presents, but you will not own this guy unless you do something radically different.

To own this guy, and I mean really own this guy, you need to tap into his bank of sexual fantasies, and make them become a reality for him.

Want to know what you might get in return?

Want to know what a man will do for you if you deliver?

He will give you anything. He will walk away from everything just to be with you. And I mean everything.

Let's see if history can back up what I am saying.

A long time ago there was a dashing young man with more money than almost anybody else in the world. He was very popular, good looking, and he came from a very respectable family, and had lots of nice friends. He could have his choice of women. He was, for a time, the biggest tuna in the sea.

All the girls wanted to be with him. Of course, he went with a few, but somehow, and for some reason, it never clicked with any of them. And so he carried on being the wealthy playboy about town, having lots of fun, but getting serious with nobody.

After a while, his parents became a little concerned. They wanted him to do the respectable thing and choose a nice woman, get married, settle down, and have some kids. After all, he came from a very wealthy family, so the pressure was on him to produce an heir and a spare, and then, if he wanted, he could go and have some fun again, as long as he did it in a discreet fashion.

This is the way it worked back then, if you came from his type of background.

Well guess what, it didn't quite work out that way.

This dashing young man met a lady. She was not from his world. She was not from his class. She was not even from his country. And, she had been previously married, and was now divorced. So, in the eyes of this man's parents and family, this woman had to go. And so they put a lot of pressure on the young man to get rid of her. But he didn't.

And why was that, you are wondering.

This lady had been born in America. She had got married and then she moved to Southeast Asia. At some point in time her first marriage had failed, but she stayed living in Asia for a while longer before moving to England, where she met the man in question. No one really knows very much about her activities in Asia, and in her autobiography she hardly mentions it, but it stands to reason that what she learned while she was there made her enormously powerful once she returned to the West.

She eventually left Asia and moved to England. She met our dashing young bachelor, and she bewitched him completely. She did such a good job on him that he gave everything up to be with her for the rest of his life.

The man I am talking about was the future King of England. Prince Edward. And the woman's name was Wallis Simpson. Prince Edward was first in line for the throne. But because Wallis Simpson was a divorcee he could not marry her. Well, he could marry her, but then he could not be King. So the silly romantic fool renounced the title, said he would not be King, married the love of his life instead, and then moved to Paris to be with her. They remained happily married for the rest of their lives.

So how did all this happen? How is it possible that the course of history in the most prestigious and important and wealthiest family in the world can be changed in this way? What power did this woman possess and use to such astonishing effect that the man who would be King chose to live with her instead.

I will venture a good guess. He fell in love with the way she made him feel. No other woman had been able to do that until then. And experts on this matter say quietly that it was the tricks that she learned in the Far East that gave her the power over him. The things she learned there she used to great effect back in the West.

The ways of the Geisha and the like, where women are taught how to please a man, is something that is missing in today's Western society. Too many women's magazines write endless articles about how every woman is entitled to be beautiful, entitled to a happy marriage to a wonderful man, entitled to wonderful children, and entitled to a big house, entitled to lots of money, entitled to a fantastic sex life. Some magazines proclaim proudly that today's woman is also entitled to have an affair, and gives advice about how to have one.

This might be so, but judging from the statistics which say that more than half of all first marriages fail, and almost three quarters of second marriages fail, and the millions of people signed up to online dating websites, it is pretty clear that something isn't working.

What did Wallis Simpson do for Prince Edward that made him walk away from everything to be with her, and what did she do to make him stay with her and provide for the rest of her life.

Chances are that she tapped into that part of his brain where he kept the dark stuff. And she played her part better than anybody else could, or had done previously. She wasn't concerned with being a goody two shoes, and she wouldn't deny him something on the grounds that it "wasn't nice". My money says that she did anything and everything that he wanted, and she did it with gusto.

Take the example of Jerry Hall and Mick Jagger. As the lead singer of the Rolling Stones he could have any woman he wanted. And yet he settled down with Jerry, who is supposed to have said that she gave Mick what he wanted every morning so that he didn't need to look for it any place else.

Contrast these sets of behaviour, of Wallis Simpson and Jerry Hall, with too many women today, who let themselves go physically, and give up on sex and on pleasing their man once they have a ring on their finger.

If you want to catch a big tuna, and if you want to keep him, then have sex fast, have it often, and do it dirty, just the way he likes it. If you do that then you will own him forever. If you don't then he will look for it elsewhere. Of that, you can be sure.

21. Just some fun

In my part of the world, practically every girl you meet wants to be an actress. Well girls, here is your big chance to hone those acting skills and try them out on a real live audience, and a paying audience at that.

Your role is to play the part of the good time girl, happy to enjoy a bit of fun with a nice guy, but marriage is the furthest thing from your mind. You like your independence, you don't need a man for money, in fact, you aren't really all that materialistic anyway, and you like the simple life. While many girls you know need the five star treatment to feel loved, you just like to go with the flow, wherever that is, whatever that means doing, just as long as it's fun. So it is the company of the guy that you are with, rather than the company he keeps or where he keeps it, or even the company that he works for, that interests you.

Got it?

Now remember that if this guy has half a brain then he will not be easily taken in by this charade, not unless you play your part well.

If he is a big tuna then he will be intelligent and therefore suspicious that you might be after him for what he has and can provide for you, rather than his personality, charm, and character. Of course he would be right to be suspicious, but there is no sense in letting him know that. You like him for who he is, not what he can give you.

It is a human trait that everybody always wants something they can't have, or something that is just out of reach. When I was a kid I wanted a car. I didn't care if it was old, broken down, a bad colour, rusty, or unreliable. I just wanted a car. Any car would do.

My nephew just turned eighteen and is car crazy. His Dad promised him a car and then for various reasons he didn't deliver. I happened to have an old Honda that I didn't need so I offered it to him. He turned it down. I was at a loss for words. Here was a nice car, the sporty version with the two doors and the big engine, and it was free, and he didn't want it.

What my nephew's behaviour was telling me was that it wasn't a means of transport that he wanted, it was something else. I had wanted a car, any car; because it meant that I could go places and do things.

I asked his mother about it and she said that he wanted a Range Rover. He didn't want a car to drive. He wanted a car to admire, polish, and show off.

So although he said that he wanted a car, that wasn't the whole story. He wanted a certain type of car, and he wanted the type that was out of the reach of most eighteen old boys.

Men are the same. If they can afford a $200,000 house then they want one that costs $300,000. And if they suddenly make some extra money and can afford the $300,000 house, they won't want it any more. Now they'll want one costing $500,000.

And so it is when it comes to women. Men always want the woman whom they can't have, or at least, not easily.

Think about Tony Montana, the part played brilliantly by Al Pacino in the movie Scarface. Tony is a low life criminal from the back streets of Havana. Through ruthless cunning he rises to the top of the cocaine business in Miami. He makes a lot of money and becomes very powerful. He could have any woman from his class and station in life, but he doesn't want any of them. He wants the woman who belongs to his boss. A blond haired, blue eyed very delicate creature played beautifully by Michelle Pfeiffer.

He woos her assiduously. She looks down her nose at him and laughs. As if, she thinks, and conveys non-verbally, I would go out with you. No chance.

Her indifference drives him crazy. He has to have her. And the more she laughs at him, insults him, the more he wants her.

Well, you can and should do the same thing. But with a little more subtlety. After all, your big tuna is likely to be much more sophisticated than Tony Montana, or at least I hope so.

So when your tuna calls you and says that he can't see you until Saturday, and yet it is only Monday, just say, "ok, have fun, and see you Saturday!" And say it with as much happiness and joy in your voice as you can muster.

He will put the phone down, and think; well I got away with that very easily. And then he will start to wonder why that is the case.

Maybe she wants to see her family, or maybe she wants to see her friends, or …...maybe she wants to see another guy.

A day or two goes by and you haven't called him. At this point he is wondering why you haven't called. So he calls you and asks if everything is ok. You reply, "Yes, just great, how are things with you?" And again, you say it with joy and happiness in your voice. At the end of the conversation he is now starting to worry.

What is she up to. Why doesn't she ask me where I am and what I'm doing. Why does she sound so relaxed. And why does she sound so happy. She hasn't seen me for a couple of days, and she won't see me until Saturday, and she seems fine with that. Hmmmmm….

At this point he will start to suspect that you are seeing another guy. Questions will race through his mind. Does this guy have a nicer car than me, a bigger job, a bigger house, a bigger bank balance, or a bigger dick. Is he taller than me, bigger, slimmer, more athletic, better looking, younger, maybe he has more hair. Or is he more fun.

The questions will drive him crazy.

And all because you didn't complain and you didn't explain.

The next time you see him, don't be surprised to get a little extra attention, extra respect, extra everything.

If you act as if you don't care, that it's just some fun, you will trigger primeval male instincts that will drive the poor man crazy. He will work harder to please you than ever before.

Now be careful not to go too far with this strategy. Do not give him the impression that there is another guy. You don't have to do that. Your mere indifference will do the job for you. So don't be coy. If he asks you after a few days what you've been up to, tell him that you went to see your family, or went out with your girlfriends, or went to the gym. If he asks you what you are doing on Thursday and Friday just tell him that you don't have any firm plans yet.

At this point he will be questioning his own strategy.

After all, you are a fun girl, you are great in bed, great company, charming, and you make him feel like a king. Now what possible reason could there be for him to feel that he might have made a mistake not to see you for the best part of a week. I mean, there's no chance that you might meet somebody else in that time, and that person might shower a girl like you with attention, is there. No, of course not.

He will be calling you to make plans for lunch, dinner, and breakfast for Thursday, Friday, and Saturday.

And all because you acted as if you didn't care, that it was all just a little fun.

That is how you catch a big tuna.

22. So nice

Sounds obvious, doesn't it. Be nice to him.

But of course I'll be nice to him, I've been nice to all my boyfriends, I hear you saying.

I don't mean be nice to him occasionally, or when you want to, or when you want something in return. I mean, be consistently nice.

Let's delve into the mind of the big tuna a little. If he's still single and swimming around looking for Little Miss Perfect, it's because he's no fool, and a little picky when it comes to settling down and sharing his fortune, oops, sorry, I mean sharing his life with someone. Silly me.

This guy probably worked his butt off in high school to get into a good university, and he probably worked hard there too in order to get into a good company and get a good job that pays for the high end lifestyle, and which could pay for yours too, if you play it right.

So the chances are that he is an intelligent, thoughtful, and hard working guy. Just the ticket. I do not know many idiots who have a lot of money, unless it was inherited, but those types tend to blow their money fast and wake up after a few years broke. So your clever tuna is certainly no fool. He will have his wits about him, at least until he falls in love. That's your game, to get him to fall in love, with you. Being wise and in love don't go together too well, remember that, and work it to your advantage.

Until he falls in love he is going to be keeping his eyes open and watching your every move. And contrary to some of the advice I see being given to good ladies like you, being mean and nasty is not the way to this guy's heart. Let the other girls run that strategy if they like, but you should make sure you do the opposite. Remember that you want him to fall in love with the way you make him feel, if not you.

So be nice to him. All of the time.

You'll hear stories about how Courtney was a real bitch to Justin, and that he loved her anyway. Yes, of course, that's possible. You can't really control who you fall in love with, but it is possible to control yourself when you are in love. And that's why lots of people fall in love, but they never make it down the aisle. The big tuna will have family and friends keeping an eye out for him. And if they see and hear of examples of the guy they love being treated badly by some pretty little thing, then the knives will be out for you every step of the way.

However, if they hear good things about you, and if they see you treating him well all the time, then these potential agents of destruction turn into allies, and you are moving a step closer to landing the tuna.

Being nice isn't all that hard anyway. And if you imagine that it's all part of being a professional then just do it.

Men are stupid when it comes to women, but they aren't complete fools. They know when they are being taken for a ride. There is a little voice inside that says, quietly, hey Joe, wake up, she isn't being nice, she isn't being honest, you are getting screwed.

That little voice should be saying, wow, she's a good one, and it's not an act. She's nice to her friends and family too. And she's so nice to me I can hardly believe it. Nobody has shown me this much warmth, concern, interest, and affection. I must be the luckiest guy in the world; this is the one, my soul mate, the lady I want to spend the rest of my life with.

Now let's say that he's caught you in a bunch of lies. Let's say that it's Friday night and he took you to see the ballet and then took you out to dinner afterwards. The logical progression for the evening would be to go back to your place or his and spend the night together. However, you receive a text message at 6pm inviting you to a party, and you want to go. The party doesn't kick off until about midnight, so you think, and realize that you can go to the show and have dinner, and then you can dump the guy and go to the party alone. There will be some friends there whom you want to see, and it might be more than a little dangerous to bring the tuna along because he might discover further evidence that you haven't been entirely honest with him about your other activities. So you've hatched your plan and you do it.

After dinner, you say to tuna boy, I am not going to invite you home tonight, and give no further explanation, other than an offer to walk him to the bus station and wait with him until it arrives. You give him a kiss on the lips, say good night, see you soon, and then watch for a minute as the bus disappears down the road, with him on it. Then you go to you party, alone.

You're probably thinking that you handled that pretty well. That you were a good little girl all evening, acted the part well. And then you blew it with some of the worst behaviour imaginable.

Think about it. Tuna Boy is on the bus going home alone. It's Friday night and he has just paid for tickets to a show and for dinner. And now he has bought a bus ticket to take him home, and it is only 10.30pm, on a Friday night.

You can not be serious.

After a display like that, you are never going to get it back on track.

And the silly thing is that ninety-nine acts of kindness get wiped out by one act of nastiness.

Sure, the tuna might stick around, but it will be different. He will take you out of his Category A for Likely Lasses and put you into Category D for Nasty Girls to use for Sex.

Good move, not.

A very attractive and intelligent girl called me one day and suggested we get together. I was delighted. So I asked her what date she had in mind. She suggested a date, we put it in the diary, and a day before the date she texted me to say that someone had offered to take her to a George Michael concert on our date night, so could we please rearrange. She also told me that this other guy was a very senior business executive, and very powerful.

I was simply staggered.

Up until that moment I had thought she was a very nice girl. She was very bright, successful in her own right, and yet she did some of the most appalling things possible.

Needless to say, both of these women are still single today. Both are extremely intelligent, beautiful women. And despite everything I still regard them as close friends. But they both spend their time and money on internet dating sites, looking for the perfect guy. They want a guy who ticks all of their boxes. Right height, look, degree of professional success, status, class, eligibility, attractiveness, the list goes on and on. They also want this guy to be dumb. Dumb enough not to notice how awful their behaviour is.

Well good luck with that. They are going to get nowhere until they get smart.

When it comes to treating a man well, they have no idea. Their judgment is not just off, its way off.

When you sit down with their girlfriends they'll say that they have no idea why Trish or Svetlana isn't married, and doesn't even have a boyfriend. They'll tell you that she's so nice, one of her best friends, and that she's so pretty, and funny, and the list goes on and on. Well what they don't see is how selfish, uncaring, and mean Trish or Svetlana is when they are playing the mating game.

The plain and simple fact is that if the girl is single and looks too good to be true, then she is.

Guys will be attracted to her, they might even like her, but eventually she will show her nasty, selfish, uncaring side, and the game will be over. The tuna will be off the line, never to be seen again.

It can all be different. Just be nice.

A girl who treats a guy well, all the time, can have her pick of men. They will line up and wait patiently to be interviewed. She just has to be nice to them, all the time. Simple. It all sounds so obvious, because it is true.

The lack of consideration and empathy shown by too many women makes it easy for the nice women out there to clean up. It's easy to stand out from the crowd by being nice when the crowd is being nasty. And stand out you will. Especially when other books and magazine articles on this subject actually advise women to treat their men mean and keep them keen. What total garbage.

But hey, why fight it. It is in your interest for all those other poor misguided women to keep doing a Kardashian on their men, because it means that when those guys meet you they will be bowled over by how good it feels to be treated nicely.

Try it and see. But watch out. You will soon have more tuna trying to swallow your hook than you can manage.

A friend of mine told me about a girl he fell in love with, how she was uneducated, poor, with very few prospects, but she treated him with kindness and consideration from minute one, with never a mishap, or slip-up. He quoted the late Richard Prior, who said, "she took me hook, line, and sinker, and I was on dry land!"

Well you can have the same result, regardless of what you look like, how much money you have, how smart you are, and where you come from.

Just be nice.

23. So nice to his friends

Ok, so you've found your tuna, you've listened to him tell you all about himself. You've focused on him, remembered everything he's told you, you've given him some crazy sex, like he's never had before, you've been fun, light, engaging, mysterious, and you blew his mind when you paid for dinner for the two of you the other evening in that expensive French restaurant that you know he loves.

You have been super nice to him and haven't put a foot wrong, and he's falling for you hard and fast.

He's clearly been telling his friends about you, and they're curious. Who is this girl they keep hearing glowing reports about, the girl who has captivated Tony the Tuna like nobody before has ever managed to do. Of course, they're delighted. They like Tony and think he's a great guy. And they want to protect him. They've seen too many girls come and go, and while a few of them were quite nice, it was obvious to everyone on the outside that they were gold diggers, after him for his dosh rather than for his wit and repartee.

So while they're happy that he has found somebody he likes, and likes a lot, they're not emotionally involved with you, so they're going to be a harder audience to win over. And you can't really play the sex card with them, right?

Wrong.

Of course you can. But it has to be played with care.

Let's go back to the basic principle that men are stupid when it comes to women. Just because Clive is Tony's friend, it doesn't mean that he can't be won over with a little bit of old fashioned flirting. Just as long as it is carefully done, and you don't rub it in Tony's face, it will pay handsome dividends.

You know and Clive knows that you love Tony and that Tony loves you. So it's not like anything is going to happen between you and Clive, is it. But the fact is that if you give Clive's ego a little stroke, he'll think that you and he have a special little thing going on, it will never be discussed, but it will work to your advantage for as long as you want it to.

The trick is to play this little game with the guys who are receptive. You will have to use your wily feminine instinct to work out which of Tony's friends will respond, and who won't. The fact is that some of his friends will respond. But keep it light. Give them some attention, make them feel special, as if there is a bond between the two of you, but do not take it any further. That would be a big mistake. Remember, you are using the principle whereby it is better to travel than to arrive, again. Let these guys think that there just might be a chance for them with you, of course, only in the impossible circumstance that you and Tony don't work out. Let them think that, but don't ever state it, and you will have just enlisted a few helpers to get Tony Tuna landed and on ice, ready for the grill.

Be sure to be nice to his female friends too. They will have a lot of influence. I'm not suggesting that you flirt with them, although it is not a bad idea with the right woman, but make sure you give them each some individual attention. A focused fifteen minutes with one of them at a time is worth a lot more than just joining in the crowd for some light hearted banter, although this is good too.

And the advice here as to how to treat his friends goes for his family too.

Guys love it when their friends like their girlfriend. And bizarrely, they like it when their friends find her sexually alluring too. Just as long as they know that they can trust their friends, and they can trust you. The reason why they like it is because it gives them a huge ego boost to think that everybody likes you and fancies you, but that you would never fool around because you only have eyes for him. It makes him feel like he is the Hot Tuna. And that feeling is hard to beat.

So, get his friends and family on your side and you will be half way to achieving your goal.

I saw this strategy played to devastating effect by the Rock Chick.

She was working this big tuna, and then she met his friends. In particular, she worked on two of these guys. She worked out that both of these extremely intelligent and successful men had a weak link. They were both short. And so she exploited this weakness. She knew that most short men have a complex about their height, no matter how much money and status they might also have. She played the percentages, and correctly surmised that these two men, while very good and old friends of her tuna, might enjoy a little ego stroke. And she did this by giving each of them some attention. She looked into their eyes, she listened to what they said, and she laughed at the right time, and smiled in her sexiest way when they looked at her.

While neither man would admit it, they fell for her. Each man quietly wondered if there might have been a chance for them with her, if only they had met her first. It didn't matter that she was their friend's girlfriend; they would not have done anything with Rock Chick even if the situation presented itself, or at least that's what they told themselves. The reality was that a little gentle flirting, shining her spotlight on each of them for a few minutes, and exploiting their weakness about their height, meant that their reports back to Tony Tuna about her would be very positive.

If you do this right, then everybody's a winner. Tony Tuna gets his ego stroked. Tony's friends get their egos stroked. And you get the tuna a little closer to your boat, ready for landing.

If, at a later date, you find yourself having problems getting what you want, but you already have the tuna in your net, then when the tuna goes seeking advice from his friends about what to do about you, you can be sure that they will give him advice to work harder, try and accommodate your wishes, and to work it out.

After all, if you were to disappear from Tony Tuna's life, then they might not get to see you again either...

So remember, when it comes to his friends and family, give them the light version of what you are giving him.

It will work wonders, you will see.

24. No prying

If you are playing the game well, then this part is easy.

All you have to do is let him do the talking. But the trick is not to pry. You will learn more about him by letting him talk, and by simply being a very patient, attentive listener. And everything you are told can be used by you to great advantage at a later date.

If he is falling for you, then he will want to impress you.

This means that he will tell you all about his biggest achievements, how well he did in school, at sports, at work, even with other women in his past. He will tell you what he has, what he owns, how much money he earns, where he keeps it, what he wants to do, when he wants to do it, where, and with whom.

He will become an open book. That's what happens when a man falls in love.

But it is always better if he opens the book himself, and then reads it to you.

Do not pry. Resist the temptation to ask too many questions. And certainly never ask him about money. If he thinks that you are after him for money then he will be gone. And by asking the wrong questions, his alarm bells will go off, he will smell a rat, and then consign you to the bin along with all the other gold diggers.

After all, if you play it right, you won't have to ask. And if you do ask, his answers are likely to be more guarded. Keep your eyes and your ears open, and your mouth shut, and you will have more information that way. He will be trying so hard to tell you about himself, to sell himself to you, that you simply won't have to ask.

So the guideline here is to let him tell you about himself, and not to ask.

Many years ago, I went for a job interview at Goldman Sachs, the preeminent investment banking firm. I was to be interviewed for a position as a bond salesman. And accordingly, I was interviewed by a bond salesman at the firm.

The interview went on for hours. And it was very strange, or at least very different from any other interview I have ever experienced, before and after.

The interviewer hardly ever said anything. Of course, he first said hello, and introduced himself, and then he sat back and said nothing. The silence was a little awkward. I waited for him to ask me a question about myself. When he didn't say anything I started to talk. I introduced myself, told him where I was currently working, where I had gone to university, where I was from, my age, experience, and ability. Still, he said nothing.

After I had spoken for a reasonable length of time about myself, I went quiet too. But he was better at the game than me. His silence outlasted mine. I started to talk again. I figured that if I stopped talking and if he said nothing, then it was a signal to me that he wanted me to continue, and so I did.

This went on for hours. At the end of it he thanked me for my time and said that he would be in touch.

It must have gone well because he then asked me to go to New York for further interviews, which I did.

For some time after that experience with him, I wondered about that interview, and about him. I realized that I had spoken about myself, virtually unprompted, for nearly five hours. And he sat and listened to me, without interrupting, for that entire time.

I realized that I knew nothing about him. He did not look like, or dress like any other bond salesman that I had met in similar positions at competitor firms.

Later on I was to learn that this man was the top salesperson at Goldman Sachs. Not Goldman Sachs, London, which is where the interview took place. This was the top salesperson working for Goldman Sachs. And this included their entire US operation too.

I was told that this man was a legend in the firm. That in the boisterous and frenzied environment of a busy dealing room, where it was customary for people under pressure to get a little loud and lose their cool, that this man was a model of calm. Not only that, but he never said a word, or hardly ever. Most salesmen would be busy talking into a telephone at their client. This man was always at his desk, phone glued to his ear, sitting back, and saying nothing.

The secret to his success? He listened to his clients. Instead of trying to sell them something that they didn't really want, he let them tell him what they did want, and then he said, here it is, how many do you want to buy.

This successful strategy made him a millionaire many times over before he was thirty five years of age.

You can do the same thing.

Find your tuna, then listen hard, don't pry, and you will be successful too.

25. Play it Hot

The old saying goes that distance makes the heart grow fonder. But it also means that someone else can slide into your place and work her magic while you're away. And it is also true that in many cases out of sight means out of mind.

Remember that the basic objective here is to own that guy in sixty days. If you are doing things correctly, then that will happen, on time and on schedule. But if you take a break half way through and disappear on vacation with your girlfriends, then the likelihood is that will not happen. You are exposed to all kinds of event risk. He could meet another girl. His ex-girlfriend might get a copy of this book, read it, realize what she has been doing wrong, make some changes, and there he is giving her another chance.

If you want to go on vacation with your friends then wait until your mission has been accomplished. Play it right and after sixty days you could disappear for six months and he'd still be gagging for it when you got back. But, if you take your foot off the gas and lose that vital momentum in the early days, then it could all end in tears, and then it is back to square one, and you don't want that.

There's just no point in playing it cool. Much better to play it hot instead. Keep the focus on him. Make him feel wanted. Make him feel special. Give him everything right now. You want him to become addicted to the way you make him feel, and you can only do that if you're on the scene and working your magic.

Try little surprise visits. Nothing creepy, but think how nice you will make him feel if you turn up on his doorstep one day, ring the bell, and give him a little thoughtful present. Nothing expensive or ostentatious, but something that shows that you have been thinking of him. If you pick something small up for him while you're on your lunch break, wrap it up and then take it around for him in person, he will be blown away. Do it more than once and he'll soon be yours.

If you don't do this then the risk to you is that somebody else does it for him instead. How are you going to compete with that? So don't take that risk. Make sure you are the one with the little surprise gifts. And make sure that someone else isn't doing it instead of you, while you are off on holiday or playing it cool.

Most women wait for the guy to do all the running, and wait for him to lavish her with attention and gifts. There is some idea that if you play it cool and let him chase you then it will work to your advantage. There's a sense that the guy should chase the girl, and not the other way around. There's a sense that the guy has to call the girl, rather than the other way around.

Well, just imagine how your average guy is going to feel if you do the opposite. You make sure that you are available when he does call. You take the call, or respond to the text immediately. Forget the playing it cool and making him wait strategy. That's old hat, and it doesn't work. And it doesn't work because that's how all the other girls are playing it, and that's why they spend their evenings home alone after work on websites like catch.com and billionares.com, writing the same sad lines that all the other girls are writing, all about liking a glass of wine and a good DVD at home, but how you also like to go out. Yawn.

Force the issue. Don't pay him a little bit of attention. Pay him a lot. And pay it often.

Stick around, and work your magic. Ask him what he is doing after work, and if he doesn't know then make a suggestion that the two of you go to that nice little bar that he likes to have a drink. Chances are that he will have such a good time with you that he'll invite you for dinner at the cute restaurant next door, and then you'll have had him all to yourself for the entire evening, and if you're really playing it right, the night too.

Remember that if you aren't with him, there is a risk that someone else is instead.

Every minute that you spend with him, giving him your undivided attention, is money in the bank.

Going back to Pattaya in Thailand, or Sin City as it is called, there is a rule that people either observe or break, at their cost. It's the "Four Night Rule". I prefer to call it Seduction City, because the women there have this game down to a science. They've been perfecting the method for nearly fifty years, so they should be pretty good at it by now. And what they know is that if they can manage to see the same guy for four nights in a row, then they have a very good chance of getting his brain chemistry to switch over in their favour, they'll start to develop feelings, and if they can keep hold of him for another ten days then he'll soon be sending them thousands of dollars. So they stay glued to the guy. They'll do anything and go anywhere with him, even to other Go Go bars, and they'll pretend to enjoy watching the girls strut their stuff around their shiny steel poles.

The girls there know that to play it cool means to lose.

As Buddha said, "the trouble is, you think you have time".

Well you do, and you don't. If you don't get this guy to fall in love with you, and do so quickly, then you have wasted whatever time and effort you did put into it. Chances are that if you stick with the playing it cool, waiting for him to chase you strategy, and therefore not really giving each tuna prospect your full and undivided attention, that you will end up with a series of not very interesting or rewarding experiences, and that when you add them all together, the reality is that you have spent years waiting around, waiting to be chased, and playing it cool, all to no avail.

Fun Girl did exactly the opposite. Her perspective was based on her experience with breast cancer, which meant that she nearly died in her mid thirties. She survived, but as is often the case with people who survive a near-death experience, they start to really live. She embraced life and all that it had to offer, often to excess. If she wasn't having fun then she made a change, immediately.

She told me that she had never been more attractive to men until she nearly died. With her new strategy for life, she went for it, and went for everything. As she said, she never knew how much time she had left. When she met a new guy she lavished attention on him. She saw him every day. If she liked him and enjoyed his company then she merged her life into his. She gave it a go. She went everywhere he did, met all of his friends and family, and showered him with support, love, good times, sex, attention, and laughter. And every guy she did this for fell in love with her.

It didn't matter that she didn't have a dime, that she was in her early forties, or could hardly contribute a penny to their life together. It didn't matter. The simple fact was that she gave him every minute of her day, outside work, and so he felt the full force of her attention.

Fun Girl didn't play it cool. She played it hot.

Last time I heard from her she was still playing the field, had had a lot of fun, was still having fun, all at others' expense, and had a long list of admirers who would marry her tomorrow.

So make sure you stick to your tuna like glue, lavish your attention on him, and play it hot.

26. Open and Honest, or appear that way

The fact is that a good relationship is not possible without trust.

This is not the same thing as saying that trust is enough to guarantee a good relationship, because nothing could be further from the truth. But if you do not trust your partner, and if your partner does not trust you, then it is over.

I know of situations that exist between struggling couples whereby each person surreptitiously checks the other person's text messages and emails. What's the point of that. If you are at the point where this is happening it means that the one person, or possibly both, is up to something not conducive to a healthy relationship.

I'm assuming that the reader is a well balanced individual and not a paranoid schizophrenic prone to delusion. Instinct is a funny thing. It generally serves a person well, if they take notice. All too often, however, we ignore our instinct and go with well reasoned thought, usually dictated by an unreasonable basic premise called love. Which means, if we are in love then we often ignore what our instinct is telling us and listen instead to the louder voice telling us that everything is ok when it is not.

So you can play this two ways. You can either decide to be honest and open, or you can decide to appear to be that way, when in fact, you are not.

The path you choose depends on you. There are costs and benefits to each route.

Let's say you decide to be open and honest. This is the easier way. It gives you the high moral ground, and you get to sleep well at night. It also means that he will never catch you out, because there is nothing to hide. In addition, on the assumption that he is also a well balanced individual, it means that his instinct will be telling him that you are a safe bet, someone who can be trusted, and that carries with it enormous advantages. Because he knows that he can trust you, he will. And the trust factor will further cement his feelings for you, and ensure that he is more open, honest, and trusting than he would be otherwise.

The second option is to be dishonest and closed. This is a far trickier proposition. And it carries with it substantial risk.

You just need to be caught in a single lie, and the trust is probably gone. Sure, you can try and cover it up with another lie, and another. But the additional difficulty with this route is that you have to remember what you've said. And if you don't have the memory of an elephant then that is going to be difficult.

You will find that the glass or two of wine that you love has now become an occupational hazard. In vino veritas, wine speaks the truth. And so it will be that you say the wrong thing at the wrong time once you are under the influence of a little too much alcohol.

Some people are accomplished liars. They lie easily, frequently, and audaciously. I guess practice makes perfect, so if you have been telling lies as a matter of course for your entire life, then you get pretty good at it.

Mystery Lady told me that she was a liar, and then said that everybody lies, so what's the big deal. Now this woman was beautiful by anybody's reckoning, she had a first class education, and a super sharp mind. Rather than tell lies in the normal way, she'd lie by omission. That is, she'd leave things out, omit to tell a person certain things, and think she'd gotten away with it.

With a lot of people she did. At work, with her family, with her friends, she'd tell lies the whole time and not really get penalized for it. After all, the lies weren't too important, and the relationship wasn't entirely dependent on the truth being told, and nor was it particularly intimate.

But with guys it was different. She was pretty, so she had no problems attracting men. She was smart and unprincipled, so she used to lead men on, often several of them at the same time. She had a great time being entertained by different guys in different parts of town on different nights. She rarely paid for anything.

At the age of thirty-two, when nearly all of her friends were married with kids, she was still single. Well, I say single. But she fell into the category of girl who always has a boyfriend, but who is also always single. She was good at this game as she had been playing it since she was fifteen. She always had a nice guy as a boyfriend, sometimes two, but she also went out with other guys the whole time as well. She used to say that she was looking for Mr. Perfect, and that she would know that she had found him when she didn't feel the urge to play around and cheat on him.

Her problem was that her boyfriend was inevitably thick, while her dates were not. Poor old thick boyfriend got given one line by her after another, and because he was a bit dim he bought it.

The clever guys she went out with figured her out pretty quickly, and didn't get involved beyond a few dinners and easy nights of sex.

Mystery Lady liked her wine, and because she was used to fobbing her boyfriend off with some silly excuses for her absences, and she wasn't used to the scrutiny she came under with the more attractive, intelligent, and successful men that she met, and assumed they were like her boyfriend, she was soon found out.

Tuna after tuna would come, nibble her bait, sometimes they even mouthed the hook, but because she told a bunch of lies, and gave the game away after a few drinks, the tuna were soon off, looking for someone more trustworthy.

Last thing I heard, Mystery Lady was thinking about moving to Dubai or Australia. She liked warm weather, an active social scene, and she had exhausted London in terms of likely prospects. She didn't realize that her game was tailored to a rather dumb target. Maybe she thought that she would find a rich guy who would provide for her without asking too many questions about why she carried condoms in her bag when they didn't use them, or why he had never met her friends, or who didn't mind that she was obviously seeing other men while being in a relationship with him.

Mystery Lady went down the dishonest path. As a result, she didn't sleep well at night, was always getting caught telling lies, was humiliated, and had an awful reputation as a result.

Rock Chick was much better at playing the dishonest game. She was a fantastic liar and had the memory of an elephant. But it didn't help her too much either. She was invariably found out by the more intelligent men that she dated, and after a while, and in spite of being in love with her, they left. She was still single in her early forties, a single mother, with limited career prospects, and an uncertain future.

They say that crime doesn't pay. In some cases I'm sure that it does. But it requires that a person be forever on guard, and must provoke a deep seated sense of insecurity that must take its toll in the long term.

So it is clear, even if you are super smart, remember everything, and have been telling lies about everything for years, the strategy will not pay off with the big tuna over the long term. Not unless the big tuna in question is an idiot, and has money only because he inherited it or won it through a game of chance. But even then, if he is thick, then he and his money will soon be parted. And this does not work for you unless you are in it for a quick grab and run.

The chances are that the big tuna is well heeled because he is smart, at least in business. And it follows that he will eventually figure you out if you are in the habit of being economical with the truth. Sure, if you follow the guidelines here then he will fall in love with you, and he'll do so within sixty days. But, remembering your purpose, which is to get him to fall in love so that you end up sitting pretty as the future Mrs. Big Tuna, with all that entails, then you do not want to blow it by getting caught in a series of lies.

Being honest is undoubtedly the best policy. In fact, you should go out of your way to be honest. About everything. Of course this means that certain sacrifices might have to be made, but it's all in a great cause.

Way too many women go the other way and get into the habit of telling lies of different dimensions, but it catches up with them.

And when it does, there is often no way back. Sure, you can invent some story to make it look less bad, but he'll know it's just an excuse. And then it will just be an exercise in how many lies he is willing to tolerate before he gives you the final heave-ho, and then it's back to the single scene, once again, trawling bars, signing up to internet dating sites, and looking for invitations to go on holiday with well heeled friends in case they know someone new that you can meet and lie to.

The additional benefit to telling the truth is that you'll be more relaxed, and therefore more fun to be around. The liars are always on edge, worried about what might come out, will they give the game away, and then there's the humiliation when you do get caught. The honest woman is more confident, happier, and therefore attractive.

Resist the temptation to do the wrong thing. And then you won't have to lie. Be honest and it will show, and it will make you immensely more attractive to the tuna.

It works, you will see.

27. The Sympathy Card

Let him be a Knight in shining armour.

Guys love to rescue ladies, so you will need a few stories to elicit sympathy and draw him in to your web. The truth is that any reasonable person will feel sympathy for someone they know and like who has had some bad luck. And it will focus his attention and concern on you, and further cement your developing relationship. What you will tell him will be very personal in nature, and it can't fail to work if you have followed the steps described in previous sections of this book.

The reason is that he has been having fun with you for a few weeks now, he has been getting to know you, to appreciate you, and you have kept it light and engaging, and he enjoys being with you. In fact, he now can't wait to get off from work so that he can be with you. You are that amazing to him. So much fun, so good to be with, and easy. And, the sex is great. On tap, when he wants it, and any way he wants it. And you listen to him. Not even his mother appears to take such a strong interest in him as you do.

So he is ripe.

The time is now good to take things up a notch. You will tell him something about you and he will feel honoured that you have shared this with him. What you tell him will be so highly personal in nature, that he will be convinced that you are deeply in love with him.

A little earlier I strongly suggested that you be honest with your tuna. Now I am telling you to tell him something about yourself that is highly personal, but it needs to be true, or at least needs to have a shred of truth to it. So have a think, even the most well adjusted person with the most amazing family and life so far has a secret somewhere. Now is the time to drag it out. Feel free to embellish it, really build the story. Time to get your creative juices flowing, and to put your little actress hat on too. This needs to be quite a performance. You want him to be left wondering, how did that happen, how was it allowed, how awful it must have been for you, and what a trooper you must be to have come out of it alive and well.

Oh, another thing. You are only going to tell this story once.

After you tell this story, you will not tell it again. He will assume that it is just too painful, that you can't talk about it again, that you shared it with him once, so that he could get to know you properly, and that now you know, you know. End of story.

This will draw him in big time. It will change the dynamic of your relationship permanently. He will feel special, and the relationship will become intense as a result.

So you are now wondering what you can say to elicit this sympathy, to draw him in, to get his focus and attention to be on you, and for him to want to know you and be with you even more.

Like many young girls, maybe you had a problem with food when you were in your teens. Perhaps you lost a lot of weight. You might have been taken out of school and sent to a clinic where with the right treatment and a lot of time you made a full recovery. But it might have been taken two years, and you might have been very ill during that time. Well, this is not an uncommon experience in the western world today.

You might go into the reasons why you lost all the weight. Maybe a couple of years earlier you might have had an unpleasant experience with a school teacher. You were one of the pretty girls in the class, and maybe the teacher showed you too much attention. He might have sat you on his knee during class time. He might have sat you in his lap, and you might have felt something strange, something hard in a place where it could not be. You know that you didn't like this teacher, but he seemed to like you, and you didn't understand why.

You were a very sensitive child. This upset you a great deal, and so you told your parents. Maybe they told you not to be so sensitive, to just go to school and do your best. The unwanted attention from your teacher continued. It got to the point that you didn't want to go to school at all. You refused. And finally they relented. You stayed at home and were homeschooled by your grandmother.

In simple terms, you were abused by your teacher and nobody believed you. As a result, you developed anorexia a few years later, which you managed to come through, and here you are with him today, alive, well, and happy.

This is the story that Mystery Lady used to tell.

Fun Girl used to tell her prospective tuna that she was a model when she was in her late teens. She was invited to London for a shoot, and ended up sharing a bedroom with the photographer in their hotel due to a mix-up of some kind. She told them that she was raped. Of course she went to the police and filed a complaint, but they told her that she shouldn't make a fuss because it was her word against his, there were no witnesses, there were no marks on her, and any court hearing would be public, and very traumatic, with only a very small chance of conviction, so she dropped the case.

Rock Chick told a clever story. She grew up in an upper-class family in Pakistan. Her father was a big game hunter and was often away on hunting trips with his wealthy friends and foreign clients shooting mountain goats. Her mother was rarely around either, as she was in the habit of entertaining her male friends while her husband was out of town. In that part of the world it was customary, and it still is, for a family of a certain class to have a number of servants living in the house to cook and clean. Rock Chick's story was that a certain male member of staff would visit her in her bedroom late at night when she was only thirteen years old. She said that her father would have shot the man if he had known what he used to do to her.

Another girl reels in men's attention and sympathy by telling them that her ex-husband used to abuse their two daughters.

Whatever you tell him, it has to be good, and is must evoke strong feelings of empathy in him. And it is best if it is something that he can understand, but can not relate to. Telling him a story about how you lost all your money in a start-up business where your partner stole all the funds will not work as well as one of the stories above. It simply marks you out as a bad business woman, or a poor judge of character. You have to have been a victim, not just a casualty.

This story, if he is ripe and ready for it, will draw the two of you together. He will feel sympathy for you, but because what happened occurred a long time ago, it can not be corroborated, nor is it likely to be the type of thing that he will share with other people.

The fact that you decided to share this story with him will have the all important effect of making him feel adored.

And that will make him easier to land when the time comes.

28. You want to fall in love one day

Just imagine that it was possible to buy a magic potion and with it any person could fall in love.

How much would that small bottle with its magical contents sell for?

Love is one of those things that everybody wants, but nobody can buy. The richest Russian oligarch can not buy love. Nor can Bill Gates.

Perhaps your tuna is a wealthy property developer, with projects all around the world. In his business activities he meets people all the time, and that probably includes lots of attractive single women too, for they seem to end up in occupations and offices where people like your tuna do their business.

The Virgin Atlantic airline was recently commended for having very attractive looking stewardesses. No surprise there. Richard Branson is a super astute businessman, and even if the various domestic American airlines have an obvious hiring policy that favours maturity and experience over youth and beauty, his airline does not.

Walk into any up-market auction house and you will see attractive female staff answering the phone and on the front desk. Go into the Interior Design Centre in London's Chelsea Harbour and you will see endless examples of very pretty young things looking at fabric samples, furniture, and carpets to furnish the houses of London's elite.

So where big tuna swim, in their normal day to day activities at work and at play, you will find plenty of pretty young things all putting their best foot forward.

So how come your tuna hasn't fallen in love with any of them yet. Because, it is not just about looks.

The chances are that the pretty young things that adorn these offices, auction houses, airplanes, and up market interior design businesses look good but they don't give off the right signals at the right time. Too many of them wear an attitude that puts many men off approaching them. So while the tuna might like to fall in love, it isn't easy if most of the women he comes into contact with appear cold, distant, and unapproachable.

Now imagine that he meets you and you tell him early on that you really want to fall in love.

This is a very powerful move. It tells him that you are romantic, that you want to fall in love, and be in love. And that implies that you want someone to fall in love with you too. It tells him that you are in play, and that you mean business.

And it tells him that you are not in love already.

This straightforward statement of intent will set the wheels turning in his head. And it will challenge him. Challenge him to do whatever is necessary to get you to fall for him and nobody else.

Remember, you did not tell him that you want to fall in love with him. And you did not tell him that you want him to fall in love with you. Instead, you just threw it out there that love is what you want. You did not mention money, kids, houses with swimming pools, Cadillacs, exotic vacations. Nothing. Nothing but love.

If he likes you then this will make him start to act and think differently. He will soon start thinking, ok, she wants to fall in love. Well, I want her to realize what a great guy I am and fall in love with me. And he will think he has a chance because you shared this rather personal piece of information about yourself with him. He will become more attentive, become more eager to please, and he will do his utmost to fend off the other men that he will imagine are also circling the prize that is you.

If this tuna is doing well for himself then he will be well aware of the fact that plenty of other women will be interested in him. He might like the attention, but deep down inside, he will know or at least strongly suspect that the majority of these other women are after him for his earning capacity and asset base rather than because they genuinely like him.

The result of your statement of intent, that you want to fall in love, will be to mark you out from the rest of those other women. He may even feel a little frustrated. After all, if he has worked hard to get to where he is then he is likely to feel proud of his achievements to date. And if you, unlike the other women, are not particularly impressed, then he will not be so sure of himself, that he has you in the palm of his hand to play with at his leisure. He'll be wondering what he has to do to impress you, to mark himself out from the crowd of other men.

When you tell him that you want to fall in love, he will want you to fall in love with him.

This move will shift the balance of power in your favour.

From this moment onwards, he will be working hard to keep your attention and focus. He will be a good boy, and will start to give you presents, and will start to text you more often, call you more often, and he will want to see you a lot more often too.

Remember that it is important to simply tell him that you want to fall in love. You did not say that you want to fall in love with him. Keep him guessing. And make him and keep him hopeful that you will fall in love. That is the trick here. Once again, it is always better to travel than to arrive.

After this, as long as you have done the things previously outlined here, and continue to do them, you are on the home stretch to achieving your goal, which is to own him in sixty days.

29. Understanding You

By this time you will have the tuna reasonably firmly on your hook. So it is looking good, but he isn't out of the water and into your boat just yet. There is still some more work to do.

It is time to bear down on him emotionally. The intensity level needs to go up another notch. And now is the time to do it. In fishing terms, you want to set the hook. An experienced angler does this by giving a sharp tug on the line once he knows the hook is in the mouth. Fish hooks have a nasty little barb on the end which runs counter in direction to the sharp end of the hook. When he tugs on the line, the sharp end pierces the flesh, and the barb gets pulled through, and as a result the hook becomes firmly embedded. At this point the fish is pretty much history. To escape the barbecue now requires some luck. Either the line must break by getting wrapped around something sharp, like a rock or a propeller, until it breaks, or the fisherman pulls too hard too soon and the hook tears through the flesh completely.

So now you want to give a little tug. Not too hard. Just hard enough.

You do this by telling him that nobody understands you like he does.

He will be on cloud nine.

Then you tell him that he is unique, and that while you have been let down by others in the past, that this just feels different, it feels good, that you feel like you can trust him. Tell him that he somehow seems to know you and understand you better than anybody else.

This will set the hook in him big time.

This simple thing will elevate him, put him on a pedestal, make him feel extremely special, and he will love the way it makes him feel.

What we are talking about here is equivalent in emotional terms to administering a powerful drug. Forget about cocaine. That high only lasts a few minutes, and after that you are continuously chasing the dragon, snorting more and more lines in a vain attempt to recreate the ecstasy and intensity of that initial high. Forget about ecstasy, ketamine, mushrooms, and heroin. This is a drug so powerful that it will keep the addict coming back for more for years. The addict thinks that it is free, or that somehow he has earned and deserves it. He will feel entitled to it. He will think that just as you gave it to him once, that you will keep giving it to him, forever.

And when he gets to this state with you, he is in love.

The balance of power will now be quite firmly in your favour.

So now is the time to start turning that power to your advantage.

30. You're the best

It's a simple thing, but the way to get on with most people is to tell them what they want to hear.

Basic things like remembering someone's name, telling them that their hair looks good, or that you like their shoes, or their car, or their house.

And when you get to the male female dynamic, there is nothing that works better with a man than telling him that he is great in bed. Not good, but great. And make sure that you tell his friends that he is great in bed too.

Men are suckers when it comes to sex, their dangly bits, and how good they are at using them, and it doesn't matter what the truth is, most men do not want to know. Let's go back to Pattaya in Thailand, where poor, uneducated girls from the jungle come to the coastal city to earn money to support their family. While a meal back home in the jungle might cost 5 Thai baht, or about 15 cents, it is possible for a girl who is willing to strut her stuff and satisfy the urges of a falang, a white man from the west, to earn 10,000 Thai baht, or $300 a day. And this is big money in Thailand, where a house and farm back in the village up north might cost only $5,000.

So the girls come to the coastal resort and make themselves available to the falang from Scandinavia, Germany, England, France, Holland, and beyond. And it is here where you see testament to the sheer stupidity of men when it comes to sex and love.

Countless numbers of bars are full of old men, often in their eighties, sat talking to beautiful, young, nubile Thai girls. It is not unusual for the age difference to be as much as sixty years. The girls chat to these old men, and then accompany them back to their villas, apartments, and hotels where they accommodate whatever sexual requests these old men might have, before spending the night.

The next evening, the ritual is repeated. Hard as it is to believe, these old men delude themselves into thinking that these gorgeous young creatures find them funny, attractive, and enjoy sleeping with them. And they believe this in spite of the obvious age difference, the fact that most of the men are hugely overweight, are bald, quite ugly, and often have difficulty walking.

When the men sit around the bar with their friends, you can hear them telling the most preposterous stories about what each of them did in bed with their respective young ladies the previous night, how many times they did it, and how much the girls enjoyed it as evidenced by the noises they made while in the throes of the lovemaking process.

Believe it or not, the men often state that their nubile, twenty year old bedroom partners told each one of them that he was the best, that she had never had a lover as skilled in the art of lovemaking as he. And these old farts believed everything the girls told them.

The men believed these ridiculous statements, and they loved the women for telling them.

Now imagine a beautiful young thing giving an old, fat, man the treatment. You're the best honey. Or a "James Bond" lie, Nobody does it better. Or a "Britney" lie, Do it to me one more time. Or the rather unimaginative but still worthwhile and effective, you have the biggest dick I have ever seen. You very sexy man. I want baby with you.

And guess what, these guys fall head over heels in love with these girls. And later, they get to pay the price for their ridiculous self delusion.

You can and should do the same. Don't worry if your tuna is fat, bald, old, crippled, smelly, or suffers from halitosis. Tell him he is the best you have ever had, that he turns you on like nobody you have ever met before. Don't be afraid to go over the top. Ask him how it can be possible that he is still single when he is so attractive and awesome in the sack. Do whatever he wants, no matter how bizarre or disgusting. And tell him that it really turns you on. Tell him that he is crazily adventurous, wild, and animalistic, and that you have never been satisfied by a man like this before.

He will believe everything you say.

He will start to wonder why he wasted all that time with all of those other women, none of whom really appreciated him for who he is. He'll think they were all a bunch of liars, that they were only after him for one thing, and that you are truly different.

And when you are not in bed with him, make sure that you do plenty of touch and rub with him. Put your hand on his arm, on his hand, and rub up against him like a cat. You will be astonished at the effect that it has on him.

The Thai ladies can usually get a guy to fall pretty hard in just three weeks.

Make your tuna feel like he should be in a porno with you, and you will own him for sure. So make sure that you have porn star style sex with him. And lots of it. And if you haven't seen a porno then get on the internet fast and find out what it means and what it looks like. Ask him what turns him on and do it. And tell him that doing it with him really turns you on. Sexy noises are good. So plenty of ooh aah, yes baby. And when you come, make sure you are loud.

This, my dear, is the way to a man's heart. Forget about what you might do for him in the kitchen.

31. Flattery will get you everywhere

By now I hope you are getting the message that it is very important that you make this tuna feel like he is the only fish in the sea, that you only have eyes for him, and that he is the best thing that has happened to you in your entire life.

He will now be in love with you, and so now is the time to apply the super glue which will mean that he will stick to you like a limpet.

Your next move is to make this man the center of your universe. All of the concentration and focus that went into the early stages of your fishing expedition will be used to good effect now. Everything that you learned about him, everything that he told you about himself, his wants, dreams, and desires will be replayed in such a way that he will be convinced that you are his true soul mate, and while it is possible for him to live without you, he won't want to.

You will show this man a great deal of adoration. And you will idealize him like he has never been idealized before. You will continually remind him how amazing you think he is, you will exaggerate his achievements and downplay his weaknesses. You absolutely will not criticize him or anything that he has done or does. You will support every decision and every action that he makes. To you, this man simply does not make mistakes. While others may have disagreements with him, you do not. In fact, whatever the situation, you will always take his side and have his back.

If he has a disagreement with a family member then you will listen carefully, and you will fashion your argument so that you not only agree with him, but you will encourage him to stand firm in his view, and you will assure him that he is absolutely 100% correct.

When he comes home and shares with you a certain difficulty he may have had at work, again, you will take his side, completely. If he tells you that he murdered one of his subordinates because he or she failed to deliver in some petty way, then you should tell him that he did the right thing, that the subordinate had it coming, that he or she deserved it, because your tuna is right, and he is always right about everything, and that if somebody got killed, then it needed to be done.

You must never give him the idea that you think that his judgement is or was a little off, that he could have done a better job or made a better decision, that maybe he acted without thinking, or that he was wrong.

In your eyes, he is always right, he is always clever; he is always considered in his thinking, and compassionate and fair in his actions.

Putting him on a pedestal in this way will superglue his love to you.

You must always adore him. Look into his eyes. Do it a lot. And focus your eyes so deeply into his, that he can have no doubt about the fact that you adore him to his very core, that there is simply nobody else who has ever done it for you like he does. Give him the look. The look that says that he means everything to you, that nobody and nothing else matters to you, except him and the two of you.

You need to worship him, to make him think that he is your God, and you are his Goddess. That together you can make anything happen, and that above and beyond anything else, that you will be at his side, his loyal servant, lover, friend, confidante, and supporter until you die.

If you do this and do it convincingly then you will own this guy. Not for a week or a month, but for as long as you want. He will be transfixed and addicted to the drug that you are giving him. And he will keep coming back for fix after fix.

The late American President, Ronald Reagan, had such a woman. Her name was Nancy. She gave that man the look. And she gave him unwavering support, love, affection, and loyalty. And she gave it to him until the day that he died. If ever there was a woman who could give a master class in "Adoration, Worship, and Idealization of Your Man", it was she. This course should be taught at Harvard, because the importance that it can serve in a woman's life can not be over estimated.

Find your tuna, and then hit him hard with the look, maintain it, and you will be set for life.

Some women might feel that they shouldn't have to behave in such a way in the 21st century. That it is demeaning to look up to a man in this fashion, and that it should not be necessary, that the man should love them for who they are and what they are about, rather than because they play act in a subservient role to get what they want.

Well, it is a free world, and to each his own. But the fact is that it is intelligent to act in this way, because it serves a purpose and the best interests of the woman. Just look at Angelina Jolie. How do you suppose she stole away America's most eligible married man from America's sweetheart, Jennifer Aniston.

Let me tell you, Brangelina came about because of the way Angelina made him feel, and because Jennie probably thought that she didn't need to act that way. Checkmate. Game over. And all because Angelina understood the game and played it well, and Jennifer didn't.

There's no point standing on a train track and looking down the line where you can see a train coming at full speed and not moving out of the way because the train schedule says it shouldn't be there. The fact is that if the train is heading your way, then you either move or you get run over.

So let the other women complain that they shouldn't have to play the game and be nice to their man. Let them keep telling themselves that they have been nice enough, that he should adore her, idealize her, and worship her. That he should be putting her on a pedestal, and giving her the look. Should should should. Keep dreaming. Meanwhile, you do it first. And you will see that he will return the treatment with interest.

That is the point. With so many women backing off and playing it cool, there is a tremendous opportunity to jump in there, do the opposite, and reap the reward as a result. Sure, it takes a little more effort. But the more you put in the more you will get out.

I'll wager you that Jennifer Aniston would do anything to know where she went wrong, and what Angelina did right to win the man. No doubt she'll say that it was nobody's fault, that it just ran its course, that it got tired and it was time for both of them to move on. But deep down, when she is being honest with herself, she'll know that she had America's biggest tuna on her line, and she let him get away. She will know that she did something wrong. Whether or not she will be honest with herself and admit it, and change her fishing technique is a good question.

Paul Newman, the Hollywood icon, famous for his good looks and easy smile and blue eyes was married to his wife Joanne Woodward for many years. This is not common in Hollywood. Leading men and Hollywood starlets are like butterflies, landing on one attractive flower for a while before flying off to land on another, and then another, seemingly ad infinitum.

When he was asked why, with all the other very attractive and far younger actresses that he had worked with over the years, he had always remained faithful to his wife, he replied that he preferred to stay home and eat steak rather than go out for a hamburger.

I have no doubt that Joanne Woodward showered Paul Newman with adoration and idealization, and worshipped him and flattered him until the day he died.

And it is only common sense and uncommon intelligence that says you should too.

32. Showing interest

At this point, you're doing pretty well. You've got this big, beautiful tuna on your line, you've set your hook, and now comes the time to reel him in, to make him yours for good.

The method to use here is to show interest in him. Or at least make him think that it is the case.

There is hardly anything more seductive for a man than a woman showing interest in his life, his problems, issues, his personality, character, his self. Remember that you have already played the sex card, and it worked well. And it is still working for you. But now you are moving the game up onto a higher plane. After all, in truth, he can get sex anywhere. If he is well heeled then a visit to any five star hotel in a metropolitan area will provide him with easy access to commercial or semi-commercial sex. So the sex you give him will be great, of course, but the real pull will be the sex plus your interest in him.

Imagine this guy's life before you came along. He works hard, takes a load of risks, goes home at the end of the day, and then calls his friends and meets them for a drink, to watch a football match, play some golf, or watch some television. All very guy oriented. And let me tell you about guys, how they interact with each other. It is all about banter, and having fun, drinking beer, and keeping your guard up. If a guy is having problems of some kind he is unlikely to bring them up as a point of conversation down at the local pub either before or after the football match, nor is he likely to mention it while preparing to hit a drive on the 12th hole at Wentworth on a Sunday afternoon.

Nope. It doesn't happen that way with guys.

Guys keep quiet about their problems when they're with their guy friends.

Case in point, breast cancer among women versus prostate cancer among men. Which cancer gets more airtime? Good lord, women can't wait to tell everybody about their breast cancer screening, their diagnosis, their treatment, and how they feel every step of the way.

When Fun Girl was diagnosed with breast cancer, the magazine she was working for asked her to write a weekly column to keep the nation's female population up to date with her latest news on the subject. Guess what happened. The circulation increased by 30%. When she had her picture taken in bed with all her hair gone after chemotherapy, it went up some more. The audience couldn't get enough.

Even to this day, if you walk into a pub or restaurant in a far flung corner of the United Kingdom, complete strangers, women I'm talking about, will come up to her and start conversations with her about her breast cancer and about theirs. It is not unusual for the entire group of women to then go off to the bathroom together to compare scars.

When Angelina Jolie has a preventative double mastectomy, not because she has breast cancer, but because she believes that she is at risk of developing it, it is world wide news.

When Fun Girl's cancer was in remission, and there was no further risk of her dying, or at least not imminently from breast cancer, the column was cancelled. She then had a spell as their Agony Aunt, but as entertaining as that was, it didn't pull in the readers like a good story about her breast cancer.

Returning to men. Can you recall a single story anywhere about a high profile male celebrity who has or had prostate cancer. I suspect not. And yet a male friend of mine who works in the medical field said to me, "Blake, we're all going to get prostate cancer and probably die from it, that's a fact".

Men do not talk about their problems easily, if at all, to their male friends.

Hence the opportunity for you.

Guys want to talk about their problems, their insecurities, and their fears. But they need a willing audience. And they want the information that they reveal about themselves to go nowhere.

If your tuna has enough confidence in you then he will tell you virtually everything. You will end up knowing him better than his mother does, and even better than he knows himself.

But in order for him to have that confidence in you, he needs to perceive that you are not only an attentive listener, but that you are interested too.

Show him that you are interested, that you really care, and this tuna is close to the boat and ready for the gaff. Oops, for you non-fishing ladies, the gaff is the big metal hook that the fisherman uses to grab the fish when it is next to the boat so that it can be pulled clear of the water and into the boat.

If you can get him to feel confident enough with you so that he drops his guard and reveals all, then you are doing really well.

It is nearly the point of no return. Once he does that it is almost as if an internal switch goes off in his brain, and it makes moving backwards or retreating virtually impossible.

You must show interest. The question is how.

Now is the time to ask some questions. Not about money, or the specifics of the problem. That might be useful, but it will not do the trick as well as asking him about how he is feeling. He'll tell you all about his problems, and you will listen. While your advice is no doubt very good, it's not what he is really after. In most cases, he has already made his mind up about what to do, and he is unlikely to take your advice in terms of a course of action. Remember, he is a man. Think about when we drive. We never admit that we've made a mistake and gone the wrong way, and even if we do, we never reverse and turn the car around. We don't do it because we are men. We are not programmed to admit we're wrong and to then do something about it. So we'll just keep driving in the wrong direction and look for another way back, which usually involves driving in a great big circle. It takes more time that way, but we don't have to admit we're wrong, so it works better for us.

You will ask him if there is anything that you can do to help. You will ask him if he is ok. You will ask him for updates, and each time that he gives you one, you will ask him again if there is anything you can do, and you will ask him again how he is feeling about it all. And you will listen quietly to what he says.

You are going to do for him what his best male buddy can't do. You are going to listen, and you are not going to tell him what to do, you will not make fun of him, you will support him, and you will let him know that you are there for him now and that you will be there for him later, any time of the day or night. You will tell him that he can call you anytime, anytime at all, even at three o'clock in the morning.

And when you speak to him the next day, you will ask him again how he's doing, is he ok, is he feeling a little better.

And as a result, he is going to think that he has finally met The One. This girl is awesome. She's pretty, sexy, great in bed, fun to be with, all my friends like her, she likes to do the things I like to do, she's easy going, and she's interested in me, how I'm doing, how I'm feeling.

Wow, what a girl.

At this point, you are nearly home and dry.

33. Center of Attention

So you're a single mother, you have a three year old daughter. She means the world to you. She's the first thing you think of when you wake up in the morning, and the last thing you think about when you close your eyes and go to sleep at night.

Time for a little change.

Of course you love your daughter. She's sweet, adorable, and everything you live for.

But you now need to act as if your tuna holds top spot.

Here's what will happen if you don't. Hot Tuna will take you out for drinks and dinner. Sooner or later the conversation will turn to what you're really most interested in, which is your darling daughter. You'll probably tell him all about her day at preschool, her runny nose, and you'll tell him that her father hasn't seen her for weeks, isn't that shocking that he doesn't care, and you may even mention that your ex is behind on his payments to you, and that you're really stressed.

You'll have another drink and then really get rolling with all your troubles and worries. You may even tell Hot Tuna all about how your ex cheated on you while you were visiting your mother with your daughter, and give him all the sordid details about the long brown hair you found in your bed when you returned home after your three week trip, and how he didn't even have the decency to clean the place up and get rid of the evidence of his adultery.

Then you'll tell him about the phone calls you've had recently with your ex, and how his new girlfriend is pregnant, and how you're annoyed because this means that some of his money is going to go towards supporting her and her baby, instead of it all going to you.

You will tell him about little Courtney's upcoming birthday party, the cake you have ordered, the dress she is going to wear, and how the party is going to be held outdoors so you hope that it doesn't rain.

Then there are her doctor's appointments, how you are going to get there and back without a car, and the question about the health insurance premiums and whether or not they are still being paid by his company or whether you and your daughter are off his policy.

He will listen quietly. And the whole time you are talking about your daughter, he'll be wondering what happened to the fun, mysterious, attentive, sexy girl that you once were, and he'll be wondering if and when the old you is coming back, or if she's gone for good, and now he's stuck with a woman who only talks non-stop about a three year old child that he doesn't know and doesn't want to spend his evening talking about.

Sure, sure, there are many ladies out there who will be thinking, hey, I've listened to him and know all about his problems, now it's time for him to listen to me.

And those women will still be single mothers until they change their tune. Those women will take their precious children to preschool, and pay for them to be there and to be looked after until six o'clock in the evening, which is what time they can get there after work. Then they'll go home together and Mommy can spend the next two hours making her precious little thing dinner, and then give her a bath before putting her to bed at eight o'clock.

So let's add it up. Single Mom works all day to pay for strangers to look after her daughter from 8am until 6pm. So the strangers see her daughter ten hours a day. She sees her daughter for about three hours a day.

That is the price Single Mom really pays for the liberty she takes when she spoils her chance of a better life with Hot Tuna by talking about something he doesn't want to hear. Yeah, sure, Tuna should listen to you too, right. Why? What purpose does that serve? It does not enable you to spend more time with your daughter. It guarantees that you spend less time with her.

So, be smart.

When you are in the company of Hot Tuna, make sure you talk about things that are of interest to him. And unless you have hit the jackpot and uncovered a type of man that I have not seen or known before, that does not include talking incessantly about a child he doesn't know that was fathered by another man. Simple. End of story. That is the way men work. And if you really believe that Hot Tuna is different, then carry on testing your theory. My money says that as soon as he's got another good prospect he'll be gone. History. Never to be seen again.

Let's say you take my advice and go down the other path. So you go out with him and make him the center of your attention. You make it all about him. His day, his problems, his kids, his family, his issues, his everything. And you do that every time you go out together.

Remembering that by doing this you will own him in 60 days. So that means listening to him, and making him the center of your attention for 60 days. After which, he will be utterly and completely beguiled.

And once he is utterly and completely beguiled by you, you will be in a position to do whatever you want. But you have to get there first. And you have to earn it. No, you don't deserve it as if by some God given right. And no, you are not entitled to it either. You have to earn it. And it really isn't all that hard. So keep your stories about your daughter to yourself, and give your mother a call in the morning and talk about it for three hours, if you like. But do not spoil a good thing by talking to the Hot Tuna about it. Even if he asks, keep it short. He is only asking out of politeness. And if you keep any explanation short then it will only add to the mystery about you, which is always a good thing.

The trade-off is simple. If you believe that Hot Tuna should listen to you talk about darling Courtney all night, then you get to see darling Courtney for three hours a day, and the strangers get to see her ten hours a day. And you get to spend all day working in an office doing a job that you really love to do.

Conversely, if you elect not to talk about Courtney while you are out with Hot Tuna, then you will get to see her for ten hours a day. You won't have to work. And you can go to the gym for those spinning sessions that you used to do when you had a partner who provided everything.

So, to quote the Cambodian philosopher again, the renowned J Pow, it is "up to you".

Do the math. Work out what's really important to you. Is it really sensible to insist and believe that the best thing for you and your daughter is that he takes an immediate and unnatural interest in her? Or is it better for everyone if you keep your daughter's life separate from the business of landing the big tuna, until he's landed, gutted, and on ice back on dry land.

Play it smart, make him the center of your attention while you are with him, and both you and your daughter will benefit immensely. And he will take more of an interest in your daughter if you don't force her down his throat. I know of many examples where the woman played it smart, and things went from Single Mom to Mrs. Hot Tuna, and he ended up loving the daughter as his own, and paid for her entire upbringing and education.

Play it smart, or someone else will.

Make him the center of your attention, at least while he is in your company.

34. Craving and Sacrifice

I saw an interview with Jerry Springer where he was asked why the people who came onto his show did it.

In case you aren't aware, Jerry Springer is the TV show host largely responsible for inventing the global phenomenon that is called reality television. The networks love it because it makes a lot of money. There are no highly paid movie stars or celebrities who need their huge appearance fees, five star hotel rooms with the walls painted in their favourite colors, or private jets to get them to and from the television studio.

Just plain normal people, often uneducated, but with a story to tell. And they come cheap because they don't need appearance money.

So why do they come on the show and air their dirty laundry for the entire world to see. Is it because they want their fifteen minutes of fame that Andy Warhol described, or is there another explanation.

Jerry Springer's explanation was that the people who came onto his show just wanted to be heard. He said that many of them did not have high powered jobs, they didn't run companies, or manage lots of people. They didn't go to meetings where they were asked what they thought about this or that. He said that nobody ever asked these people what they thought about anything.

They make a phone call, free of charge to a TV station, and suddenly they're on TV. What? It's that simple? Why, they ask. And they're told that the viewing audience wants to hear their story. Are you serious, people want to hear my story, they wonder. Can this be real. Nobody ever wants to hear my story, they're thinking. They feel flattered, but still wonder if it can be true.

But then, just to prove it, a limousine picks them up at their house, takes them to the airport, and then they're on the plane, all paid for by the television network. From there they get picked up and driven to a hotel where they stay the night, free of charge. The next day, they're driven by limo to the TV studio and they meet Jerry. Jerry. The Jerry guy on TV, the famous guy. They're actually talking to Jerry. And this famous guy wants to know all about them. He wants to know everything and he listens real well too. And he's a nice guy. Wow. This is nice. Ain't nobody treated me real good like this before. So I'm going to do exactly what Jerry wants, and I'm going to tell my story real good.

The rest is history. Jerry's show has been running for thirty years, which makes him one of the world's greatest entertainers, almost in league with Oprah.

What works for Jerry will work for you.

I'm not comparing your tuna to your typical Jerry Springer guest star.

Of course not. I hope not. But human nature is human nature. And your tuna will love to tell you his story every bit as much as Jerry's guests love to tell theirs.

And as long as you crave hearing his stories as much as Jerry loves listening to the stories of the people on his show, then you'll be doing just fine. Jerry built a reality television empire on his ability to listen to the people on his show. Now Jerry's a super intelligent guy. Extremely active in politics, a famous liberal minded activist, and an all around good guy. Everybody loves Jerry. But to be honest, sometimes you have to wonder how he does it. I mean, the people and the names are all different, but the stories are all the same. Surely, after five years of hearing the same old stuff he's got to be pretty bored with it all. And after ten years, come on. It's like Groundhog Day, everyday's the same.

Jerry's been doing it for thirty years. Thirty years. And like Frasier Crane, he's still listening.

So, if Jerry can do it, listen to the same old stories for thirty years, how long can you do it for. How much is it worth to you.

Kate Moss apparently said that "nothing tastes as good as skinny feels".

And she has built an empire on the sacrifice that she's made as it relates to food. Forty years old, and still good enough to grace a copy of Playboy magazine, and paid well to do so.

We're talking about a little sacrifice here. Jerry has listened to the same old story for thirty years. Kate Moss hasn't had a decent meal in twenty years. Look where they are as a result.

You job is to do something similar, but in a much smaller way. Your job is to listen to his stories. Just listen. Not talk. Your job is not to listen to one of his stories, and then it's your turn to tell one of yours. That's a no no. You aren't going to build an empire like that. Not even a little one.

Listen to the stories your tuna tells about himself, his favourite car, his brand of golf clubs, why he prefers Budweiser to Miller, why he likes his steak cooked well done, why he hates the Yankees but loves the Red Sox, why he needs a new hip but can't decide whether to get it done straight away or wait for a few years.

If Jerry can do it for thirty years, you can do it for the 60 days it takes to get this guy hooked and landed. After all, it's all in a good cause, which is you.

If you go for a late night walk along the Beach Road in Pattaya, Thailand, at about four in the morning, you'll see dozens of ladies lined up looking for customers. It's strange, because prostitution is illegal in Thailand, and yet you'll see half a dozen hookers standing next to each other, and then you'll see a policeman dozing while sitting on his motorcycle, just a few feet away.

And I wonder when I see this. I mean, it's a third world country, the drains stink, and the rats are scurrying around all over the place at that time in the morning, and you have to wonder why the girls do it. Firstly, it is illegal. Secondly, it can hardly be safe to go back to a hotel room with a complete stranger to have sex. Thirdly, there is the risk of disease. So why do they do it.

Options.

They do it because the other options available to them are even less palatable. Maybe their only other option is to work in a restaurant or a bar, where they might earn 3,000 baht, or a $100, in a month. Even in Pattaya, Thailand, that isn't going to get you very far. Or another option is to work on a rubber plantation, slaving away in the fields under the tropical sun for twelve hours a day for a pittance, or working in a motorcycle factory making foot pegs. Your job is to operate the same piece of machinery for twelve hours a day. And if you slip up and get a finger caught in the machine, then it's too bad for you. Health insurance provided free as part of the job. Forget about it. The reason why poor Thais look after themselves, eat well, stay slim, is because they can't afford to get sick. So they decide that the best option, all things considered, is to go down to the beach road at 4am and sell their bodies.

Your options are hopefully and fortunately much better. You can listen hard, and you can end up with a tuna that will provide for you and your child. And unless you are extremely unlucky, your tuna's stories are likely to be at least as interesting as the ones that Jerry listens to all day and every day.

It's a small sacrifice to make. And you get to eat a lot more than Kate does. And you don't have to work in a motorcycle factory, or sell your body down on Beach Road to get what you want.

So do it.

Listen to his stories. He'll no doubt have opinions about politics, religion, sports, cars, beer, how to raise children best, the meaning of life, how the west was won, the universe, WWII, and he'll love telling you all about them.

Just another small sacrifice to make to get you where you want to go. As the old Bob Dylan song says, we all have to work for somebody.

The sacrifice you will make here, the minutes and hours you spend listening to him telling you about everything from the best barbecue sauce to why he thinks Porsches look best in silver will be the best investment you will ever make.

No doubt he will have a lot of ideas. Ideas how to make money. Ideas about buying a certain vacation home. Ideas about the stock market. Ideas about where to go for the weekend. Listen to them all, and appear to be hungry for the next one, whatever it happens to be.

He'll lap it up, and it will deepen his emotional attachment to you. Try it, and you will see.

35. Reeling him in

So far, it has been mainly about him.

At this point, and all because you have followed the steps outlined in this book so far, he absolutely adores you. It doesn't matter what anybody else thinks or says to the contrary, you are the best thing that has ever happened to him. And because you make him feel so damn good, he will do anything to preserve things exactly as they are. And he will ignore anything and everything that doesn't fit, or conflicts with the image that he now has of you in his head.

It is now time to turn it around a little. But it has to be done in a subtle fashion.

He is hooked, and the hook is in deep.

I've seen examples of men who are in this state who are oblivious to the truth, and who simply do not want to see it and all because they are in so deep. Things that you would not believe.

There is the example of the good looking thirty year old Australian who had his heart crushed by a girlfriend. He took a vacation to Thailand where he met a young Ladyboy. For those of you who may not be familiar with this phenomenon, a Ladyboy is a Thai man who undergoes a series of operations to change his sex and to become a woman. For some reason, there seems to be a large number of them in Thailand, and frankly, you would be hard pressed to tell the difference between a Ladyboy there and a regular Thai female. The old saying amongst the falang is that the really pretty and attractive Thais are the Ladyboys and not the women. Sure, it's hard to believe, but if you take a trip there one day you will see what I am saying.

Anyway, so our young Australian heterosexual man has his heart broken by an Australian girl, and so his mates take him on holiday to Thailand, thinking that with a little bit of luck, he'll meet a pretty young Thai or Russian girl, have a holiday fling, and it will take his mind off the ex-girlfriend back home.

Well, the theory worked. The only problem was that it worked too well. And it was complicated by the fact that he fell head over heels in love with a twenty year old Ladyboy. And he wasn't ashamed of it either. He posted pictures of the two of them together all over Facebook. He took her home to Australia to meet his parents. They were horrified. And he was constantly showering her with everything from brand new iphones to expensive seafood dinners for her and her extended family. She soon had a bank card issued by his bank and could draw money out of his account as she liked.

So you're wondering how this could happen. It happens because the Ladyboy made him feel good. And when someone makes you feel really good, then it doesn't matter where you come from, what you look like, or, sometimes, even what sex you are.

Your judgment becomes suspended, once the hook is in deep.

So your aim is to get your tuna to swallow the hook so far down his throat that there is absolutely no way that it will come loose when you start to reel him in.

And if a young, poor, uneducated, Thai Ladyboy can do that to a macho, heterosexual Australian, then you can do it to your tuna.

Another example is the situation where another highly intelligent man fell so deeply in love with a woman that he ignored the fact that he caught a sexually transmitted disease from his girlfriend not once, not even twice, but three times, and even then he still persevered with the relationship. In fact, he was so fearful of losing the relationship that he didn't dare confront the girlfriend over the issue of faithfulness. He so wanted to continue feeling the way that he did when she was being nice to him that he overlooked the obvious fact that she was cheating on him. When a man will do that, you know that the hook is in very deep.

Rock Chick had a boyfriend so in love with the feeling that he experienced when being with her that he ignored some powerful anecdotal evidence that she was fooling around on him, to the extent that he also caught a sexually transmitted disease from her, but bought her excuses rather than demanding the truth and an explanation.

The story is that she went away to Mexico to attend a wedding of one of her friends. As happens at events like that, in a beautiful location, love is in the air, she met one of the other guests, a good looking guy, and she had a fling with him for the two weeks that she was there. Needless to say, she kept this quiet and didn't tell her boyfriend at the time, who was busy working back in London.

Anyway, holiday now over, she returns to London, and resumes her normal day to day life. She had her hook buried deep into the boyfriend in London. So much so, that he decided to surprise her one weekend by buying new living room furniture for her apartment. He takes the Monday off and arranges to have the furniture delivered, all without her knowledge. While he is setting everything up nicely he comes across some loose change and some receipts that had fallen down behind the old sofa. The receipts were for items purchased in a pharmacy in Mexico, during the time that Rock Chick had been away at the wedding. And there it was, plain to see, a receipt for some aspirin and some KY Jelly. The boyfriend asked her about the KY Jelly and why she bought it, and she told him that the bride to be used lots of the stuff and so she bought some for her because she was running low. A good excuse, but come on. If that hook had not been embedded halfway down his throat then he would have walked out the door then, never to be seen again.

But, and because of the way she had made him feel up until then, she got away with it. He stuck around, and she continued to play him for the sucker in love that he had become.

So you see, the drug that you have administered by employing the techniques previously described, will enable you to now turn the tables, and do virtually anything you want. He may want to do something about it, but he will be powerless to do so.

He will not want to upset you and upset the apple cart for fear that you might withdraw the supply of the love drug that he is now addicted to.

You are now in an immensely powerful position.

And so it is time to reel in his attention and concern even further.

You do this by subtly transforming your interest in him over time.

It is no longer all about him, it will become all about you, but he will be hard pressed to notice the difference. You will still be interested in him, but you will no longer be interested in what he is interested in, because you will now be interested in things that are of concern to you, and not the colour of his Porsche or his ideas about how to redecorate his apartment. Your interest becomes his exclusive interest in you, what he can do for you, rather than what you can do for him.

So the game has now changed.

In the beginning you gave him everything. And he loved it. And now it is time to reap the reward of that sacrifice. He will now do anything to get it back to where it used to be. You will still show interest in him, his ideas, his thoughts, his concerns, but you will be especially interested in them when they relate to you.

When he talks about ideas for a vacation for the two of you then you are really interested, and you treat him well. When he talks about redecorating your apartment, and buying you some nice furniture then you are really interested, and you treat him well again.

It is like the experiment with Pavlov's dogs. This guy has been well trained by you, he has learned that if he talks that you will listen and he knows that it makes him feel really good when he is with you, and so he will now do virtually anything to keep the good times rolling.

And they will, just as long as he continues to behave. You will reward him just as long as he takes an interest in you and what you want, and over time, he will come to believe that he should be thinking of you, that it is perfectly fair and reasonable for him to show more interest in things that concern you, and so he will do it.

Rather bizarrely, the net effect of the tables now being turned, whereby the focus is now on you and what he can do for you, will make his feelings for you get stronger and stronger. The guy who had all the power only a few weeks ago, when it was all about him, is now in the back seat. It is now all about you.

The tuna is now only yards from the boat, and he is ready to be landed. But first you need to tire him out a little bit....

36. Tenderness, at a price

Your tuna is now addicted to your love. More specifically, he is addicted to the way you make him feel when you are being nice to him. And he will do anything to keep that feeling going.

Have you ever been to one of those shows where the animal trainer rewards the animal with some food when it performs a certain trick in the right way? Think about those giant water parks where they have those enormous killer whales housed in those small swimming pools and where the trainers get the killer whales to do all kinds of tricks in return for a few handfuls of fresh fish.

Those little ladies manage to control the actions of a multi-ton mammal in return for a few morsels of food.

And they do this by training these intelligent animals through repetition. Do the trick well and you get some fish. Do it well again and you get some more fish.

This is rewarding the animal for positive behaviour. The old fashioned bear trainers did it the other way around. They would chain a bear to a stake and then beat it with a stick until it performed correctly. In this case, the reward was to be left alone.

So either method works. You might think that the animal being trained would prefer a positive reward rather than simply not receiving a beating for doing the right thing and behaving according to the trainer's whim, but the jury is still out on that one. Too many trainers of killer whales held in captivity for the amusement of a paying audience end up killing their human trainers for it to be a fluke or a one-off incident.

According to the famed Oxford educated zoologist, Desmond Morris, human behaviour is not so different from animal behaviour. In fact, he argues, an awful lot of human behaviour is very similar to that you see exhibited by animals. In his excellent book, "The Human Animal", he gives explanation as to why we humans behave the way we do, even explaining that monogamy is not natural, that it runs counter to the way we are instinctively programmed. He explains why we have multiple sexual partners. And he explains who they are, how they differ, and what purpose they all serve the human species in its seemingly complex mating game.

If you accept that a highly intelligent animal like a killer whale can be trained to perform tricks in return for a few fish, and if you accept Desmond Morris' central idea that we are not really very different from the animals in the way we behave, especially when driven by the mating instinct, then it is natural to conclude that your tuna can now be easily controlled by you. Either through a positive reward, or, as the bear trainer does, the cessation of a good beating, or its equivalent.

The point here is that you can now call the shots.

If your tuna does what he is supposed to do, then he gets a reward. Otherwise, he gets nothing. Or, he gets the treatment. You will show him that you are not pleased. It is up to you.

So you are now in transition. Up until now, your tuna got the friendly and nice you all the time. He was positively rewarded all the time. When he was talking about himself and you were listening, he got a reward. You, being lovely and adoring, all the time. But now, you are different. The tap is not always on. Your love doesn't gush out and pour all over him 24 hours a day. Now the tap can be turned off. And back on. But the only person who can do this is you.

When your tuna swims where you want him to swim, the tap will be on. You will treat him with exquisite tenderness. He will be so happy, the old you is back, just like it used to be, and he will be happy beyond belief. He will want more of the love drug tomorrow too, and the next day. And he can have it, but only as long as he treats you in the way that you want. Otherwise, the tap gets turned off.

Mystery Lady was good at this game. She loved her luxury Caribbean vacations, and she liked to go there in the high season. February in London is not great weather-wise. It is cold and blustery, and it is dark by 5pm. A perfect time to go somewhere warm. But, of course, everybody wants to go then, so the flights and the hotels are expensive. And although she has a very respectable job working for a top interior design company in the best part of southwest London, she doesn't earn a lot of money.

But that isn't a problem because she hasn't paid for a vacation in years. She gets an endless stream of well heeled tuna to pay for them instead. So it's Barbados in February, South Africa at Easter, Bermuda in June, and Ibiza in August. All five star resorts, all paid for by someone else.

She's so good that these tuna will do anything to keep her happy. She told me that upon arrival at her hotel in Barbados she took one look at the room, said nothing, pulled a little face, and her tuna immediately scurried off back to Reception to organize an upgrade to a penthouse suite. Of course, he paid for it, despite the money troubles he was having at the time. And she let him. Didn't offer to pay half, or even anything.

Of course, after that, she was as sweet as pie. Listened to his boring stories about his family, heard all about his problems with his graphic design company for the umpteenth time, and then accommodated his similarly boring sexual demands while she fantasized about the sex she'd actually had with a complete stranger who'd given her a line of coke in a nightclub she'd been at the weekend before.

She could do this until the cows came home, as she had been practicing the art for years. She'd worked out by the age of fifteen that men could be easily trained to give her what she wanted, and all she had to do in return was appear to be nice and to provide the type of sex that they wanted.

Mystery Lady was unknowingly behaving in the same way as the girls hanging out at 4am on the Beach Road in Pattaya, Thailand. The only difference was the price. Price in Thailand is a few thousand baht until the tuna is hooked, at which point in time it rises to a thousand Euros/dollars a month. Price in London charged by Mystery Girl is made up of drinks and dinner in expensive restaurants, and then expensive vacations, once the tuna is on the line.

As they say in Thailand, "same same".

It is easy to make a mistake here. Too often, when the tuna is on the line, a woman can pull too hard, and the line can break, or the hook gets torn out of the mouth of the fish, and then he's gone. Proponents talk of the "treat them mean and keep them keen" school of thought on this subject. It can work for a while, but eventually the tuna will get sick of it and he'll be gone.

It is much better to reward good behaviour with some kindness. It will make him try harder. And he will believe that if you aren't happy then it is his fault, and he will look to make amends and give you what you want.

If you are mean all the time then he is likely to conclude that you are a bitch and so it becomes much easier to walk away.

So, train your tuna to realize that good behaviour on his part, as determined and outlined by you, will result in you showering him with the love and attention that got him hooked in the first place.

Do this well, and you can do it for years.

He'll be jumping through hoops, and performing tricks, and he'll be happy to do so. Just as long as you treat him well in return.

37. Pull Back

When you think of a diamond you probably think that they are expensive, and that they are expensive because they are rare.

Diamonds are beautiful, they're apparently a girl's best friend, and as Shirley Bassey used to sing, they last forever. But guess what, they aren't rare. In fact, they're very common. A big company in South Africa has an enormous stockpile of diamonds, and they control the price by controlling the supply. They know that if they put too many diamonds into the market at any given time then the price will drop. So they ration the supply of diamonds, and the price stays high as a result. They've been doing this for years, and it works very well. People mistakenly believe that diamonds are a rare commodity when they aren't. In fact, it is possible to make a diamond yourself. All you need is a piece of coal and a strong vice. In fact, you will need a very strong vice. But if your vice is strong enough, all you have to do is put your piece of coal into it and then apply pressure. If you apply enough pressure then the black piece of coal will turn into a diamond. It's true. Big industrial companies do this all the time and the diamonds that they make are used to make tools that cut things like glass and ceramics, anything where a really hard substance is needed to cut another hard substance.

If you want a genuinely rare stone then there are much rarer gems like emeralds and rubies. These can not be made synthetically in the same way that diamonds can, but most people don't know this, so they succumb to the clever marketing campaigns of the South African diamond supplier, and pay a high price for an artificially rare stone.

It is now time for you to do the same thing.

Your tuna has never been happier. He's finally met the woman of his dreams. She makes him feel better than anything, and he can't get enough. He doesn't see his friends so much anymore because he is always with you. And you've got him well trained to do the things that you want him to do.

So it's now time to crystallize this happy partnership.

If he's like most men then he'll be loving things just the way they are. He's having fun, you're being super nice to him, the sex is great, and he's never had anyone take such an interest in him before, so he's addicted to your love.

But, what's his is still his, and what's yours is still yours. And he has a lot more than you do. And you're still paying a stranger to look after your darling daughter while you're at work doing a job that you hardly love. You'd much rather be a stay at home Mom, living in a nice house provided by your go to work Husband. That's the way it's supposed to be, right? Isn't that the way it was when you were growing up? Your Mom stayed home and your Dad went to work every day. That's the way it used to be. And then this whole women's liberation thing happened, and now it seems that the result is that women go to work and raise their kids, alone. How did that happen you're wondering.

And it has become the norm. The stats say that in the USA and Western Europe more than half of first marriages fail. So there are a lot of single Moms out there in the work place working hard to make ends meet, often while her ex and father of her child does his best to make himself scarcer and scarcer, coming up with every excuse under the sun to avoid making alimony and child support payments.

You do not want to be in this situation for long. It's too much work, your standard of living will be low, which is why you want to land your big tuna.

So, now that you've got him hooked, it's time to make him realize the value of what he has, and what life might look like if you weren't in it.

It is time to pull back.

You are going to ration the amount of attention that you show him in exactly the same way that the South African diamond supplier rations the number of diamonds they put into the market each year. And the effect will be the same. The value of your love will increase. Just as it does with anything where the demand remains constant and the supply suddenly goes down.

When you pull back, he will panic. This will be a big change from the way things have been for a few weeks now. Prior to this moment you have always been there for him. So generous with your time, your interest, your concern, your support, your sex, it has been an incredible period in his life. But now he suddenly realizes that, unlike the proverbial diamonds, it may not last forever.

Suddenly there is a very real risk that all the happiness he has felt might be at risk of disappearing. There's now a real chance that for some unknown reason you might disappear from his life forever, which means back to going to the pub with his friends, weekend golf, and solo sex.

And all because you pull back. Not a lot, just a little.

You explain to him that things might have gone too fast, that you are getting in too deep, that you are worried about getting hurt because it's just a fling for him, that you've been very badly hurt by guys in the past, and that you just can't do that again, it's just too painful. Of course you explain that you have very strong feelings for him, that he gets you in a way that nobody has ever done before, but it's just all terribly risky for you, that you couldn't survive another terrible break-up, and that it might be better to see a little less of each other rather than run the risk of getting terribly hurt again. Of course you'd still love to see him when you can, that you aren't saying good bye forever, that you still want him in your life, but that maybe it is time to consider where you are, that it started out as just a little harmless fun, but that now it is so much more than that for you. And you are scared. Scared for the feelings you have, and scared because you were in a bad place before you met him, but now you feel so much better, and it's all because of him, and that makes you very vulnerable.

And then sit back.

Have you ever seen a grown man cry? Well just watch, because it's going to happen. In the words of Justin Timberlake, this guy is going to cry me a river. He is going to cry worse than he did when his dog died. Worse than he did when he broke his leg. And a lot worse than he's ever cried before over a girl.

So be ready for it. And let it happen. And then walk away.

It's now time to let the situation ferment a little. So don't rush right back into it. Give him some time and space to think. It will have the effect of pushing up the price of your love, to a brand new stratospheric level.

This guy is going to go crazy. The mere thought of not seeing you, not being with you every day will send shivers down his spine. Remember, he is addicted to your love, in exactly the way that some people become addicted to cigarettes, alcohol, gambling, or drugs. And he will not like the thought of not getting his daily fix of your love. If you have followed the steps here religiously then this guy will find it extremely hard to stay away from you, even if he accepts your explanation and understands that it is probably for the best from his perspective too.

But the fact is that he is not making sensible decisions any longer. He is hooked. And he is in fantasy land. A land where the two of you live together in perfect harmony, where you listen to him, support him, entertain him, and never criticize him. Everything he does is perfect, you laugh at all his jokes, crave listening to his opinions, and look at him adoringly. What's not to like. But now this amazing woman needs to go away. He simply will not be able to let this happen, even if he knows intellectually that it is the right thing to do.

So it will not happen. He will not let you go.

Your tuna is now still in the water, but it is knocking up next to the boat. You can look it directly in the eye. And you can see its streamlined body glistening in the water just feet from where you are.

The tuna is ready for landing....

38. Unavailability

He may give it a few days, go quiet on you, and wait for you to break the radio silence. But it won't work.

In the first thirty days or so it would have worked. He liked you, and he liked being with you. After all, he was having fun. And if you were doing it right you were giving him porn style sex. The kind of sex that was unimaginable for him until he met you.

Remember that Christian Grey character, well your tuna got to be him for a few weeks, and he absolutely loved it. He will have told his brother, his friends, and even the mechanic who did the oil change on his car the other day.

But while the sex was great and he was having a blast with you, you hadn't given him the full treatment. You hadn't combined all the sex and fun stuff with the adoration and the idealization. You hadn't put him on the pedestal yet. And so a pull back then would not have had the same effect. He'd miss you, and miss the sex, but it would not consume him. The feeling would soon pass, and he'd get on with life and just chalk it up to experience.

However, you're more like fifty days into this thing with him now, and in his head and in his soul it has taken on a life of its own. Now it does consume him. And when you're not around he'll be wondering what you're up to, where you are, who you're with, and what you're doing with that person, and it will be bothering him a lot. He'll be wondering if you are shining your light on someone else in the way that you used to shine it on him. And he'll be wondering about the sex thing too, are you having it, with whom, and where.

So, in a little while he'll get in touch with you. He'll be quite casual about it, but he'll suggest that you meet up some time. You will agree. That's a good idea you'll say. And he'll suggest a date.

Whatever he suggests doing, and whatever date he suggests that you do it on, you say that you can't do it. You'd love to, but you have a busy schedule already booked, so it will have to be next week, and not before.

He may try and suggest meeting sooner rather than later. But you must not agree to it. You're just too busy with things that can't be changed. So you agree to see him next Thursday, and leave it at that.

You do not text him. Not unless he texts you. And even then, just keep it polite and friendly. And don't be in a hurry to reply, and don't engage in numerous texts that go on late into the night.

The idea here is to be unavailable. Now is the time for it.

He has got to experience what it feels like for you to be practically gone. And he has got to wonder what you are doing instead of being with him.

Of course, his imagination will run rampant. And all of his insecurities will play out. He'll imagine that you are being wined and dined by a taller, funnier, smoother, wealthier, and more generous and more sophisticated guy than himself. And he'll be green with envy.

Play this well and you can run it for a long time. And like wine and whisky, the ageing process makes the end result better.

Mystery Lady played a guy like this for an entire summer. She pulled back and became unavailable. And every time the tuna got in touch and suggested meeting up, she was always fully booked seeing friends who were in town from far away places, or she was out of town on a work assignment, or she had family obligations, sick relatives, or was feeling unwell and needed some down time to get better. Her excuses were always plausible, but they both knew she was doing other things and seeing other guys, but neither person would bring it up, and he didn't ask the question. That would have been too humiliating. So she made up her excuses, and he pretended to buy them.

But inside he was hurting. Hurting because he loved Mystery Lady, and hurting because he couldn't see her. And she knew it. But she didn't care. She kept her mind on playing her game, which was to land the big tuna. She was good at this game, and she knew that once she had a tuna on the line like this, that she could put the fishing rod down in a holder for a while, and pick up another rod and play the tuna she had on that line a little too. The tuna she was playing certainly had an inkling that there was another tuna in the water not far away that had a big hook in its mouth too, but there was nothing either fish could do about it.

Mystery Lady played her various tuna, but never ever let a tuna know for sure that it had competition. And the tuna played along and deluded themselves that they were the best tasting tuna, that it was only a matter of time before she would realize that and decide to drop all the other rods and grab the one that he was on instead and reel him in for good.

She told me about a time when the lines got crossed and two of her tuna did get to know of one another. It wasn't pretty. Tuna 1 was in a bar in south London and bumped into Tuna 2. Tuna 2 knew about Tuna 1, but not the other way around. Oh dear, it seems that Tuna 2 told Tuna 1 that he had been seeing and having sex with Mystery Lady for over two years. The problem was that Tuna 1 had been in a relationship with Mystery Lady for the last five years. And Tuna 1 was shocked to learn that Tuna 2 had been to Mystery Lady's apartment, had had sex with her there, and knew the layout of the apartment like the back of his hand.

This did not go down well.

But guess what. Mystery Lady made up an excuse, said that she'd only met Tuna 2 recently while she was in separation mode from Tuna 1, and denied having sex with Tuna 2 for the two years prior.

Tuna 1, because he was in love, decided to believe her, even though he must have suspected that she was lying.

He decided to let it pass because he thought that if he made a big deal about it then there was little to no chance of seeing her again.

Mystery Lady had successfully played Tuna 1 and Tuna 2, plus a number of others that neither of them knew anything about. And she played them all by getting the hook in deep, then pulling back, and then becoming unavailable.

Being unavailable, after giving a tuna the pull back explanation works well because it makes the tuna competitive. Instead of swimming off to find someone else, his interest in her actually increases. And it increases because of the nature of the pull back explanation.

When amateurs at this game pull back they normally do so in a hurtful fashion by blaming the tuna, telling them that they aren't interested because the tuna is too young, or too old, or is already married, or is too poor. When an expert like Mystery Girl pulls back, she tells them that she needs to do it because she doesn't want to get hurt, that the tuna is simply amazing, that she'd love to stay with him, but that it can't happen because she can not run the risk of another broken heart.

So Mystery Lady pulls back and becomes unavailable because the guy is too attractive, too great, and because it would be too painful to lose such a catch as he.

The difference is method is subtle, but the difference in the effect is not.

In the case of the amateur's pull back, the tuna swims away and thinks that he has lost nothing. Yes, he fell in love with her, but he realizes that she is a nasty piece of work, and he'll get over her quickly. With Mystery Lady, the tuna swims away, reluctantly, but he doesn't go far, and he keeps swimming back, and he remembers her well, and he remembers the way she made him feel, and he longs for her as a result.

After that he goes to parties and meets lots of other women. But as Sinead O'Connor sang, nothing compares to her.

Sure, he'll have a good time without her, but he'll be constantly comparing the new women he meets with Mystery Lady, or Fun

Girl, Rock Chick, or Thai Dancer, and they will always come up short in comparison.

I am not suggesting that you become unavailable so that you can play some other fish at the same time. That is best left to experts like Mystery Lady, and remember, she's been doing it for over fifteen years now. And that can lead to another problem that you don't want to have.

Too many choices.

Experts at the game like Mystery Lady get so good at fishing for several tuna at the same time that they end up falling in love with playing the game so much that they lose sight of the objective, which is to get the tuna in the boat, back home, and then on the barbecue. And eventually, even though the tuna is completely blinded by love, he figures out that he is being played, and then will quietly give up and slip away, realizing that it is no prize to end up on her barbecue after all.

So be unavailable, but don't be horrible. Don't insult the guy's intelligence with excuses that are so far fetched that he retaliates in some way.

Another girl who thought that she was good at the game was wondering why she was still single at the age of thirty-five, despite stunning good looks, a pole dancer's body, and a first class brain. The mistake she made was to work on the basis that her tuna were not as smart as she was. So when she went unavailable, her excuses for not being able to meet on a Friday or Saturday evening ranged from she was "too tired" to she "had to work on her job application". And the reason why he never met any of her friends was "because she didn't have any".

She may as well have called him a brainless idiot to his face. Her tuna took it all in but started playing her back. Instead of falling in love, he hardened his heart, but continued to enjoy the first class sex that she offered.

After two years, during which the relationship went nowhere towards her aim of marriage because of her less than skilful fishing technique, it was she who walked away, with not much to show for the experience.

Make sure that when you are unavailable that you do so in a respectful fashion. Insulting the guy's intelligence with see through excuses will get you nowhere, they may even cost you.

Be unavailable in an intelligent way and respectful way and you can start reaching for your gaff and landing net, because you tuna is about to be landed.

39. Push Away

It could be that your tuna will be so in love with you by now that being unavailable is not going to work. He may not allow you the space and time that you say you want and need. Remember that when he doesn't see you, he is going to feel the same way an alcoholic feels when he can't get a drink, or how someone who is addicted to cigarettes will feel if he can't smoke. But worse. He is likely to feel extreme withdrawal symptoms, and often, he will feel an irresistible urge to contact you and to meet you. So you may need to go to Plan B. And Plan B means it is time to push the tuna away from the boat.

In the last chapter I described a situation where Tuna 1 got wind of the existence of Tuna 2. In fact they met each other because Tuna 2 became angry because he couldn't see Mystery Lady, and so when she became unavailable, he assumed that she had gone back to her ex-boyfriend, Tuna 1.

Tuna 2 was a feisty Latino type, a good looking young man with a fiery hot Italian temperament. And he was in love with Mystery Lady big time. After a while of him hearing her excuses as to why she couldn't see him until next Thursday, he decided to do a little investigating. A little Facebook research and he soon figured out the name of her supposed ex-boyfriend, and he went looking for him in all the local hang-outs. After a little while he found him, and the showdown commenced.

Both guys found out that Mystery Lady had been telling them both a bunch of lies.

And they each discovered that she had been seeing them both at the same time.

Ouch. That hurts.

The funny thing was that while they were having their little confrontation in a south London pub late one Saturday night, with each guy laying claim to the affections of Mystery Lady, she was curled up in bed with Tuna 3 up in Chelsea.

And even crazier, the knowledge that Tuna 1 and Tuna 2 had about each other made her more attractive to each one of them.

Of course, she told them each what they wanted to hear, that while it was true that she had seen the other guy once or twice recently, it was only because she had been forced to do so, not because she really wanted to, because she really and deeply loved one and not the other.

And then she pushed them both away.

You see, the problem was that both Tuna 1 and Tuna 2 were madly in love with Mystery Lady, but they weren't coming to her yet on her terms. She had to go to Plan B so that she'd get what she wanted from both of them, and she did that by taking the drug away from the drug addict.

Timing is everything. If you push the tuna away from your boat before the time is right then it is quite possible that you'll never see him again. It's as if you suddenly discover that the hook that you used was defective in some way, or the knot that you used to tie the hook onto your fishing line was improperly tied. The result is that the hook or the line breaks, and the fish is free.

So be very careful to push your tuna away only when you are absolutely sure that the hook is secure and the line is fastened properly.

Tuna 1 and Tuna 2 had both sworn their undying love to Mystery Lady, as had one or two other Tunas that neither of them knew anything about at the time. She had been playing Tuna 1 for a long time. And in the time that she had been playing him, his fortunes had taken a turn for the worse. His business had declined, and it wasn't looking like it was going to rebound any time soon. In addition, Tuna 1 came from a close family and his mother and brother didn't like Mystery Lady very much, and the feeling was mutual. Of course, they felt that she had too much power over Tuna 1, and they were right. Unbeknownst to them, Mystery Lady had no interest in living in a quiet south London suburb in close proximity to her future mother and brother-in-law. She wanted to live somewhere exotic, somewhere warm, and in a style that meant she could enjoy the easy life courtesy of the successful endeavours of her husband. Tuna 1 was not looking like he was going to come up with the goods. So she pushed him away. She knew that if she had done her work well that Tuna 1 would say anything to get her back. But she wasn't going to be convinced with words. It was action she needed to see. So she told him that she wanted to live abroad, and she needed a partner with enough money to fund a lifestyle for them both which would allow her to stop working and perhaps have a child or two. And then she dumped him.

Tuna 1 went crazy. Making her happy meant leaving the city and country that he had been raised in and which he loved. It meant taking a risk and setting up a new business. And it meant providing for her and a child at the same time. It meant liquidating all of his assets in the UK to start a new life somewhere more to Mystery Lady's liking. And it meant making a break from his mother, brother, and friends, and moving to Dubai or Australia so that she would be happy.

That's a big ask. But guess what, after the pull back didn't work, she employed the push away and it happened just as she had planned. Tuna 1 agreed to do anything and everything she wanted, in return for the pleasure of her company, and regular supplies of her love drug.

And all the time that she was playing the push away with Tuna 1, she was seeing Tuna 2, and setting him up for the big play too.

Oh, and yes, she was of course still playing the field and dropping new fishing lines into the water with baited hooks, just in case she hooked a really big tuna while she was landing Tunas 1 and 2.

Amateurs at this game often go badly wrong when employing this tactic to close the deal. Either they play the card too soon, or they are afraid to play it at all.

If they play it too soon, before the hook is really set, and before the guy is well and truly addicted to their love, then they run the risk that the guy just gives up. And if they don't have enough confidence to play it, even though they're pretty sure the hook is well set, then she never gets things done on her terms. She will always play second fiddle to him and what he wants. She'll often live in his shadow, the engagement ring will never come, the marriage will never happen, nor will the children or the asset transfer into her name.

When the time is right, and you're sure you've done everything correctly as outlined in this book, then be bold, and pull back. If he doesn't pester you then leave it like that for a while. Lie low. And wait. Be prepared to be patient. If you have played it well then it is only a matter of time before you will hear from him. And as long as he blinks first, then you have been empowered.

If you pull back and he comes after you like a raging bull, swearing his undying love, but nothing more, then you go to Plan B, the push away. Ask him politely to leave you alone. If he tracks you down and discovers that you have been seeing other guys, don't deny it. Tell him that as far as you were concerned the two of you were on a break, so you have done nothing wrong, and were well within your rights to see other guys. You could even tell him that you naturally assumed that he was doing the same thing, as you two were no longer properly together.

The pull back will work with a lot of guys, and the push away will work with the others.

And the net effect will be that both types will respond by giving you exactly what you want.

You will end up with the terms dictated by you, and paid for by him.

40. The Chase

So you have him where you want him now. He's promised to deliver everything that you want, and so he thinks that everything will return to normal as a result. Wrong. You aren't going to let that happen.

As a result of following these guidelines you now have the upper hand. Your position is now very powerful. You've got him wrapped around your little finger, so now is not the time to do anything to let that change.

After all, you've worked hard to get where you are today. You've behaved perfectly, and been the perfect girlfriend for nearly two months for this guy. He is now so in love with you that he's ready to do anything for you. And that's the way you want to keep it.

Remember earlier on when I said that the person who loves the least has the most power. Well that person is you, and don't forget it. All that nonsense about equal partnerships, what a pile of garbage. Either you wear the trousers in this relationship, or he does. That's the way it is.

Take a close look at many relationships in America and Western Europe that last and you will see that either the husband or the wife has the upper hand. Rarely is a long lasting relationship a result of the decision making lying equally in the hands of husband and wife. Of course the media will want you to believe differently, but it's a lot of hot air.

You want to be in charge.

Sure, let him charge around and climb the corporate ladder and provide for you and your kids. But when he comes home from the daily battlefield he will report to the real Commander-in-Chief, you.

Before he buys a new car, he will ask you. Before he makes any vacation plans, he will ask you. Before he makes any investments, he will ask you.

But the only reason he will do this is if you get him in the habit of doing so. And so it starts now. You aren't going to spell it out for him, but this is the trade-off. As long as he tells you everything that's going on, how much money he's making, where he keeps it, and what he's going to do with it, then he gets his regular supply of your love drug, or else.

And you want to get him in the habit sooner than later. And you want and will demand to see evidence that this is the case. Or once again, he will not get his fix.

The tuna is only worth catching if it tastes good. There are lots of other big fish in the sea, but the tuna is the king. And it's the one you want. But when you get it in the boat you don't want it flapping about all over the place. Remember that it has been swimming in the sea for a long time, and it feels comfortable for it to do so. Lying on the bottom of your boat at your feet will be a new experience for it, and so you will want to get it on ice fast.

The trick here is never to go back to how it used to be in the early days with him, but never to tell him that those days are gone for good. Instead, the trick is to keep him believing that as along as he makes you happy that you'll continue to treat him like a king. Once again, it's better to travel than to arrive. Of course, you will, because that's your end of the deal. But, because the demand for your drug is high, and because you control the supply, you will want to ration that supply very carefully.

And so you let the chase begin.

In the drug world it's called chasing the dragon. The first line of cocaine provides the greatest high. After that first line, each successive line provides a nice pick me up, but nothing in comparison to line number one. However, the cocaine addict does more and more cocaine, always looking to feel the same way with each successive line as he did with the first. But it never happens.

Your tuna will be like the drug addict. His memory of how you made him feel will be ever present in his mind. And because the memory of the good times will be so powerful, he'll do anything to feel that way again. And it is your job to let him feel that way, and to let him believe if he'll just do this or that, then he'll feel that high with you again.

You don't have to do a lot to get him to do what you want. He just has to believe that if you aren't happy then it's because he isn't delivering the goods and that there will be consequences as a result.

And the consequences are that he might not get to see you until he starts to deliver.

This might sound a little cruel, and you might think that it shouldn't be this way, that there should be a nice equal partnership where neither person has a hold or power over the other. Well you are welcome to try that approach if you want. Perhaps you have already tried it a number of times with other guys, and it didn't work out too well.

Well now is the time to embrace reality, and to make it work for you, instead of living in the land of self-delusion, being on the wrong end of the power balance, and paying a heavy price for the experience of getting it wrong.

Let him chase you. And don't let that ever change. As long as you realize the value of who and what you are, and realize the value of what you offer him, then he will value it too. But if you give it away freely, or without limit, then he will take it for granted, and you are doomed.

Sometimes you can use little tricks to remind him just how powerful you are, and that he isn't the only one who values you correctly, that there are others waiting in the wings to pick you up if he drops you.

Rock Chick would often arrange to have a drink with a guy friend without telling her Tuna. Then she'd give her tuna the cold shoulder for a few days, until he complied with her latest demand, at which point she'd invite the tuna along to join her and her guy friend for a drink after work. The other guy was invariably a married man whom she'd had sex with at some point in the past, although she never admitted this to her tuna. She told me that it was very amusing to watch the two guys socializing with one another, neither too sure exactly what was going on, or

what had gone on, and she wasn't making it easy for either one
for them.

Later on, she'd go home with her tuna, and he'd be in a mood to
do anything to please her.

He wanted his love drug fix, and she had given him a not so
gentle, but very well delivered message that her drug was good,
and that it was expensive. And he chased her dragon, and paid
the price to do so.

So, let him chase you, and remind him from time to time that
your drug is expensive because it is the best, and he will keep
coming back for more.

A very good way to promote this chase is to make up little
excuses as to why you can't meet him on any particular night.

The best and surest way to drive him crazy, and to really tire that
big tuna out so it is easy to lift him out of the water and into the
boat when the time comes, is to tell him that you're "going out
with your girlfriend for the evening". To comfort an old friend
who's feeling down.

And as the great Eagles track says, "But he knows where you're
going as you're leaving, you're heading for the cheatin' side of
town". Even if it isn't true, let him think that it might be.

This works for you in a couple of different ways. Firstly, it gives
you room to work on a prospective new tuna, just in case things
don't work out with this one. And it makes it much more likely
that you'll land the tuna, and on very favourable terms to you.

This elusiveness that you are now practicing is a very powerful
stimulant to the chase. He wants to be with you, but he can't call

you a liar and say that you are out with other guys when you aren't with him. To do that would make him appear to be paranoid or delusional, or so he will think. And so you might tell him. So he'll keep quiet. But inside, his insecurities will be boiling over, and he'll know or strongly suspect that you are seeing what else is out there in the deep blue sea for you.

Be careful not to play this hand too aggressively. You don't want him to get fed up and thrash about so much that in the ensuing melee the line gets broken.

You want to play it skilfully, tell him that you'd like to meet him but that your old friend Sarah is in town and that you would really like to catch up with her. And the following week it will be Lisa that you have to see, and then some other friend a few days later. Of course, it will just be the two of you girls, getting together for some good old fashioned girl talk. After all, you don't want your tuna to invite himself along. If pressed, just tell him that you'll be going for a drink and maybe a pizza afterwards. But don't commit to being in a certain place at a certain time. The last thing you want to do is to make it easy for him to check up on you.

And when you are not with Sarah, or Lisa, or Marie, just tell him that you are having dinner with your Dad one night, and with your Mom another night. And then there's your sister, and your old friend from university and the list goes on and on. You are managing to be elusive but without giving him any concrete evidence that you are up to tricks.

You can play this game for a little while, but if you play it for too long then there's a real chance that he will bolt, and swim as fast as he can in the opposite direction. And just as a fisherman doesn't want to run out of line when the fish swims away, nor do you want to play it too hard and watch him disappear into the distance, in the obvious knowledge that he has been played.

Make sure that when you do see him that you are attentive, caring, interested in him, and give him every reason to believe that you love him, and only him. That way, when you aren't with him, he'll have the fresh memory of how wonderful his time was with you, and he'll use that memory to delude himself into thinking that when you say that you're with your friend or relative, that you really are.

So, you let him chase you by being elusive, by giving him reasonably credible explanations for where you are or were, making sure that he can not check up on you, and then by being super nice to him when you are with him.

This will work a treat.

Your tuna will soon be exhausted and almost ready to jump into your boat for you, all by himself.

41. The Break-up

Well done, because if you have got this far and followed all the steps, then your fish is ready for landing.

All your hard work, time, careful thought and planning, and skilful mastery are now about to pay off. You're thinking that all you have to do is to wait for an invitation to dinner at a super romantic restaurant overlooking the ocean, with candles, a bottle of fine French wine, and an engagement ring to follow. You're probably wondering how big the diamond is going to be, and hoping that it is in a nice setting that shows the world how much he loves you.

You do not wait for anything for long.

And if the ring is not forthcoming very quickly, then it is time to take the game up to a higher level.

You walk. Out the door. As Gloria said, he's not welcome any more.

Game over, is what you want him to think. He had his chance and he blew it. If he really loved you like you love him, then he'd be down on one knee pledging his eternal faithfulness and love, and proving it with at least three carats.

And if he's still standing, and there's no ring, then it can only mean that he doesn't love you, that all his talk was just talk, that he has been wasting your time, probably seeing other women behind your back. And the whole time he was doing that, you had put your entire life on hold for him.

Tell him that, and then sit back.

Getting back to your ambitions to be an actress, well here's your chance again. Forget about truth and love and integrity. It's time to close the deal, to land your tuna. And if you ain't lying then you ain't trying.

You need to put on the performance of a lifetime. You need a performance worthy of Meryl Streep or Cate Blanchett, not Jennifer Aniston. I'm not sure about you, but I am always impressed by actors and actresses who act out different personalities in their various characters in their films. As opposed to those actors who just play themselves in every movie that they're in. Ed Norton and Tim Roth and Philip Seymour Hoffman. Proper actors.

Well you need to be one of those good actors. The ones who play a part instead of just playing themselves. You need to play the part of a woman so desperately in love, and so in need of love from this man, that you would rather walk away empty handed and broken hearted rather than just go through the motions with someone who didn't really love you.

You believe in love, and you believe that love with the right man means eternal happiness for the two of you. When you met him, you felt like he was the one, the guy you had been waiting for all your life. The guy you were scared that you'd never meet, or perhaps didn't even exist. and how when you did come along, you fell madly in love, but that intensity of love scared you, that you could hardly believe it could be true, but that you took a chance and went for it, and now it looks like it was all in vain. You are just devastated. And left wondering how you could ever pick up the pieces and start again. No, you tell him, there will be no more love affairs for you, this is just too painful, and from now on you'll just keep it light and easy with the guys you meet. It'll just be fun, nothing serious.

Of course, your tuna is already madly in love with you, and he will be wondering what's going on. After all, he's told you already that he loves you; he's told you that he's making plans for the two of you to be together, and so it will happen.

The problem is, you say, that all you get from him is words. And that you've been promised things like this before from other sweet mouthed people, and that you've been let down, and suffered terribly as a result.

You're now sure, because of his inaction, that he's just another one of those guys who promise a lot and deliver little.

And that's why it's over. You've come to say goodbye, to get your stuff, and that it's now time to move on.

This guy is going to go crazy. He will beg you not to go. He'll explain that it's all about to happen, that these things take time, and that you just need to be a little more patient.

You explain that enough is enough, you can't go on like this. Thanks, it was nice knowing you. I wish you all the best, here are your keys, and good bye.

It will take a lot of strength for you to do this, and to do it in a convincing fashion. You might think that it is very risky, that the better tactic is to do as he says, play along, be quiet, and wait. But the fact is that you must be prepared to take that risk. The only question to ask is when to take it, not whether you should take it or not. And you take it when you firmly believe that the hook is in the mouth, and it is in deep, and he is tired of playing the game, and he wants it to be like it used to be, and if you break-up when all this is in place, then he will do whatever it takes to restore things back to the way they used to be, when you were happy, and he was happy, and so he will see the next step as a very small price to pay for the dream of a happy life with you to come true.

After all, he'll think, he loves you, you love him, it's perfectly understandable that you would want to marry him, and why shouldn't he marry you. Everybody gets married, and not always to a person they love. And so in a sense you and he are very lucky, because you do love each other, so marriage is the right thing to do. So he'll quickly switch into marriage mode, and you'll soon have a proposal and a ring.

But you have to be prepared to threaten him with the ultimate sanction, a break-up. And he must believe that you are serious and that you will go.

So prepare yourself for the performance of your life, because how well you perform will determine the outcome of all the efforts you've made in the last seven or eight weeks.

When the time is right, just do it. Tell him that you are done, that it isn't working for you, and then leave. Tears and lots of emotion are good at this stage. Tell him that he is a wonderful guy, and wish him the best of success with his life, but leave him with no doubt that you are serious, and you are done.

And then just walk away.

The tuna is now practically in your boat.

42. Time to say Goodbye

After you have walked away and given your tuna some time to think, he'll get in touch with you.

He will want to see you and will suggest that you meet and have a talk. Ideally this will happen after several days have passed, during which you have managed to control yourself and have not contacted him.

Congratulations are in order. When he calls and asks to meet you, then you have won. The tuna is now in your boat. He is almost ready to be eaten.

Have you ever read one of those fancy cookbooks where the recipe calls for a marinade for some fish or meat? It suggests putting the flesh in a bowl of marinade and then setting it aside in the refrigerator for a few hours or overnight. The marinade then has time to flavour the flesh of the animal which makes it tastier once it is cooked.

Well you are going to do the same thing. Think of the words that you used in the Break-up as a marinade, and now let him sit in a bowl of those words for a few days before you agree to meet him.

And the way to frame your next meeting is to mention that you want to say goodbye properly.

This will set the meeting up nicely in your favour. He will be on the back foot from the start, and he will know that he will need to come armed with something pretty good if he is to somehow turn this around.

Remember that he is going to be desperate at this stage. He will now fully believe that you are in love with him, but that you can't go on because he has failed you in some way. And so he is now staring into the abyss of loneliness as a result, and he knows or believes that it is do or die time, or else he risks letting the love of his life, and his future happiness, walk away from him forever.

This is a loaded situation. And the gun is in your hand. And he knows what he must do to salvage the situation, and that is that he must cave in and give you what you want. Or else, you walk.

So you agree to meet up, set a time and date. Make sure the location is somewhere neutral. You certainly do not want to meet him at your house, or his. He needs to come to the meeting knowing that at the end of it you both go your different ways, and then that's it.

And when you meet him, you want to be pleasant, apparently happy and confident, but at some point you must give him the look. And that look will be a reminder of what he is giving up if he doesn't come up with the goods.

The meeting will go one of two ways. He may fail to deliver, but that outcome is very unlikely. Or he will deliver everything that you want on a plate. And if you have done your job well then you can be sure that the marinade has worked, and that the tuna is ready to be cooked and eaten.

The big tuna has been landed.

You now own that guy.

Postscript - Case Study

As part of the research for this book, I travelled from London to the coastal resort of Pattaya, located on the eastern side of the Gulf of Siam in Thailand. I was interested in a phenomenon that I had heard about from friends and acquaintances that I met while working in London's equivalent of Wall Street, which was colloquially referred to there as The City.

These hard working and intelligent men had vacationed in Thailand and had returned to London and then had engaged in the most extraordinary behaviour imaginable. They started to send large sums of money to the women they had met there, and they did this regularly, and they often travelled back to Pattaya in small groups to pick up with the same women they had met there and to whom they were sending thousands of dollars a month to support.

There were even instances of sophisticated and urbane men of this ilk and social milieu who had split up from their wives back in the UK, and had then gone on to marry these Thai women. The compliance officer of a top tier German investment bank even showed me pictures of his wedding day to a young Thai girl from a small rural village. His wedding ceremony was conducted in what appeared to be a small clearing in a jungle, in what could have been a movie set from an old Vietnam War movie like Platoon or Apocalypse Now. And I could even see the bride's family house amongst the trees, which appeared to be a shack with a corrugated iron roof. And Mark was sitting there, in a dark blue suit and tie, cross-legged on a dirt floor, holding hands with his bride, and he looked happier than I had ever seen him during the four years or so that I had worked with him in the bank back in London.

I was astonished that such a thing could happen, and I wondered if the guy had lost his mind, or what extra piece of information about this situation was missing that could explain how such a thing could have happened. After all, Mark had divorced his wife of ten years, with whom he had three children back in London, and he had married a girl with a background and lifestyle about as far removed as possible from what he had always known, and he was delighted with his decision.

It didn't seem to me to be a mid life crisis thing, there were no sports cars or the like. And while the girl was not ugly, she did not appear to be the type of girl who had the obvious physical attractions that would explain what was happening here. To be frank, she looked quite plain, so this was not a thing being driven by looks or obvious sex appeal.

So as part of my research into the allure that I understood these simple women from Siam apparently possessed, I went there to see for myself.

If you have never been to Pattaya I urge you to do so if you are open-minded and of a naturally curious disposition. What you will see might shock you, but hopefully you will be pleased that you went, and I can assure you that it will be a very memorable experience.

The Mayor of Pattaya's aim is to build this once small fishing village into the Miami of South East Asia. Tourists visit from all over the world, but it is especially popular at the moment of writing with Russian visitors. Thailand and Russia do a lot of trade, and part of the deal between the two countries means that Russians can easily travel to Thailand without any visa restrictions, and so they visit in droves.

As Thailand is about a three hour flight from Russia, you could think of it as being equivalent to the route between New York and Miami. So some Russians go to Thailand for the weekend. The international airport in Bangkok is enormous; it is very modern, and highly efficient in transporting large numbers of visitors in and out of the country. I have not experienced the lengthy delays at immigration and passport control there that I have had in the USA. And from Bangkok, it is an easy and direct 120 kilometre taxi ride down a modern highway to Pattaya, at a cost of 1,200 baht, or $35.

Thailand is very warm, as you would expect from it being located only about 15 degrees from the equator. As is often the case in places at this latitude, daytime is relatively restrained, for it is at night when the place really comes alive. And there is nowhere on earth that I know of that comes alive in quite the way that it does in a place called "Walking Street" in downtown Pattaya.

It is along Walking Street that you will see the most extraordinary display of human adult life in all of its vibrancy and variety, and it puts places like Las Vegas to shame in comparison. You will see everything from five pound lobsters on ice, waiting for a hungry seafood connoisseur, a six year old pony tailed girl contorted into a perfect circle balancing on the back of her father's bicycle, to a hundred different neon signs, all trying to entice you to enjoy their particular brand of entertainment. There are go-go bars, all highly differentiated on the outside by extraordinarily beautiful young Thai girls, who could be dressed up as airline stewardesses or something similar, and all vying for trade. And their aim is to get you off the street and into the bar, which is where the entertainment really starts. Then there are the Russian competitors, with their long legged blondes, dressed up in Arab harem type outfits, outside on the street, and also to be seen writhing on floor to ceiling poles through windows on the floor above.

Then there is the phenomenon which, while not peculiar just to Thailand, has to be seen to be believed. At various points along Walking Street will be dozens of Ladyboys, the men who want to be women, and guess what, they are often not merely beautiful, they are often spectacularly beautiful, with appearances that defy the reality of their true gender. I challenge the casual observer to tell me that these incredibly convincing creatures are not women.

To be honest, apart from their voices which they can do nothing to change, the only real evidence to the contrary is their height, because they are usually much taller than real Thai females, and the fact that they are so well groomed and made-up, and have such impossibly perfect bodies, which have been made that way by numerous operations and careful diet.

The medical industry in Thailand is world class, and there are many people who travel there from all over the world as medical tourists to have cosmetic surgery. On the evidence of what you can see along Walking Street at 4am, these tourists are getting a very high quality service at a price which is heavily discounted relative to what it would cost in the USA or in a private hospital in western Europe.

The so-called fast food available there is similarly exotic, strange, and tasty. Here you can buy anything from delicate barbecued mushroom kebabs, spicy five chilli papaya salad, chicken feet and congealed chicken blood, enormous grilled prawns, to deep fried seasoned scorpions and maggots.

Sometimes it is best not to ask what you are eating and to simply enjoy it for the flavour instead.

It is to this cornucopia of visual, sexual, and epicurean delight that I came to help me understand what makes Thai women so successful when it comes to landing their tuna of the Western variety.

Of course, it was necessary for me to visit the go-go bars with all their shiny poles and high heeled dark skinned beauties, each with a number pinned to a wristband or to their skirt, and also the more subtle variation of the same, where a highly erotic show was performed by the girls, but where the emphasis was more on the beauty of the style of Thai dance that is performed there, rather than a simple and mundane western style pole dance.

As is the difference between food from the west and from the east, so it is with the dancing. Pole dancing imported from the west just seems so bland and boring in comparison to the fabulously elegant way the Thais dance with their fluid and mesmerizing hand and arm movements, which have to be seen to be believed. Like comparing a pork chop with cheese that you might find in an upscale restaurant in Florida to a spicy Thai vegetable salad made with fermented fish. Simply no comparison.

I recommend that you try and see this place before it becomes overrun by the American fast food giants who seem to have a knack for spoiling local culture with their over salted and sugared processed food and with their gaudy and tasteless branding and signage.

So into this maelstrom of excitement I dropped, fresh from a cold and dreary February London. It was on or about the second night in town that I sampled a show at a place called Angelwitch, which was located on one of the Soi, or side streets running off Walking Street. The show had a very good reputation, and it was apparently very tasteful, as was evidenced by all the couples in the crowd.

It was at this show that I met Thai Dancer, one of the showgirls. Suddenly she was sitting next to me. Just like that. Her command of English was about a degree or two north of non-existent. She was slender, dark skinned, with long dark hair as is the case everywhere in Thailand, and pretty. Not beautiful, but pretty. And she was very engaging. Somehow. It was something in her eyes that just seemed to do it.

She asked me "what you do and where you from". I tried explaining that I was writing a book and wondered if we could meet up some time for a chat. And I offered to pay her for her time. I got the distinct impression that she did not understand a word I said.

Within a few minutes a rather large and portly Thai lady approached us. Her English was almost perfect, and only bettered by her eye for business. She asked me if I "wanted go boom boom with lady". I told her what I wanted, and she simply said by way of reply, "you pay bar fine 1,000 baht, and you pay lady 2,000 baht short time or 3,000 baht long time".

So there it was. A cold hard deal. I could buy this lady for the rest of the night for $120.

Well, when I was playing golf with my brother-in-law at St Andrews in Scotland a few years earlier, and we had the choice of hitting a risky shot or playing it safe, he said to me "we didn't come all this way to play it safe and lay-up, did we". Lay-up is a golfing expression for taking the safer but less rewarding route to the hole.

Well, on that hot and humid night in Pattaya with the showgirl, I did not lay-up.

She came back to my hotel with me and stayed the night, and it was very pleasant, but the language barrier was still a little difficult. I managed to learn that she was from a place in the north called Khon Kaen in the region called Isan, a rice farming area, that she was thirty one years old, divorced, with two young children, a five year old girl called Fang, and a four year old boy called Lekke. She was shy and reserved in a way that was unexpected. But she was delightful. She gave me her number the next day, told me to call her, and we went our separate ways.

I was learning fast that the stories the girls there told the falang could be contrived, dishonest, and designed to fool the unsuspecting customer. Customer is actually the word they use for the falang whom they meet. And I was told that almost all of the girls had a Thai boyfriend or husband, and often both.

A week or so went by and I got a text message from Thai Dancer. She wanted to see me. And she suggested that we meet on the long promenade called Beach Road, which runs north south along the main beach in central Pattaya. It was a nice afternoon, almost time for my daily Magnum ice cream bar, and so I agreed to meet her. We agreed to meet at "the heart".

I had a vague recollection of seeing something like a heart on the promenade somewhere, and so that is where we met for the second time. In front of a huge red heart, where couples go to have their picture taken together. Again, it wasn't easy with the communication. Neither her English nor my Thai had improved much since we last met. But, she now had a telephone which could translate English to Thai, and Thai to English. And she knew how to use it, clever girl.

After our walk we adjourned to my abode, which was now a rather nice condo apartment on the 16th floor in a building overlooking Pattaya Bay. The view from the balcony as the sun went down was spectacular. We had a very pleasant afternoon. As before, I did not lay-up. And we spent a couple of fun hours conversing via her translating telephone. And again, she was very engaging. Clearly very much in love with her two children. She spoke to them both by telephone while she was with me. And she told me that they were back home in her village being looked after by her parents.

Later on we parted, but agreed that we might see each other again, but no specific plans were made.

And a few days later she got in touch, asked me to come to the show and to see her again. I was busy exploring the city, and did not want another evening at this particular show as I had seen it once already. So I declined, but agreed to her suggestion to meet the next day, in the afternoon, which we did. This time I was told that I had to pay a bar fine again, for the privilege of seeing her again. I was rather annoyed, as I had not gone to the show, and did not want to pay her money to take her away from a show that I had not been to. But, as the language barrier was still difficult, I agreed so as to avoid a scene.

A little while later she invited me to her birthday party with her friends, which was the next day. I felt quite flattered, and so I agreed to go.

And then she got busy on her telephone, said I had to speak to Mamasan, the portly lady at Angelwitch, the one with the business savvy. I refused. More texting, followed by the instruction that I was to pay a bar fine twice. One for today. One also for the next day, her birthday.

So now I was being asked to pay a bar fine, the price a customer pays a bar or show to take a girl away from the bar for the night, and I was being asked to pay not one, but two. Two bar fines to pay, despite the fact that I had not been to a bar, and Thai Dancer had contacted me, not the other way around. I was going off the situation and the girl pretty fast.

Being a native New Yorker from Long Island, I realized I was being hustled by the Mamasan back at Angel Witch. And so I refused to pay, and I escorted Thai Dancer out of the door. And I thought that I won't be seeing her again.

Well, she got in touch by text, and somehow made me understand that I had got her wrong, that it wasn't her fault. I strongly suspected that the Mamasan had been directing operations from her dinner table, and that Thai Dancer had been under instructions from the boss to squeeze me for money, and she confirmed that this was true.

We exchanged some texts during the next couple of weeks but didn't meet up until my last night in Pattaya. She sent a text at about 10pm to say that she was not working that evening, so could we meet up. We did. She and her friend Em and I enjoyed a great evening dancing to a fabulous Thai band, and then Thai Dancer and I went back to my apartment. I told her the following morning that I was leaving for London later that night. Of course, I expected her to take her money and leave. After all, there was nothing in it for her to stick around for any longer...

I was wrong again. She accompanied me to the Hard Rock Cafe where I picked up some T-shirts for my daughter and a friend. I offered to buy a T-shirt for her too, but she politely declined.

I then got a call from a fabulous American photographer called Brad, whom I had met there earlier in the month. He invited me to his apartment for the day as he knew that I had checked out of my place and had the day to kill before my flight later that evening.

Brad is a super charismatic guy who used to shoot covers for various high end magazines. He is a real artist, and therefore very creative. I told Thai Dancer that I was heading over to his place and invited her along. I expected her to say no. After all, she was still dressed in her black cocktail dress and sparkly shoes from the night before.

Before I knew it we were in a taxi to Brad's place. When we turned up he tells me that his Thai girlfriend of four weeks is there also. Brad has taken thousands of photographs of the most beautiful women in the world for some of the most famous magazines in the world. This Thai girlfriend of his is beautiful, but when I arrive I see that she is dressed in her usual attire, which appears to be a man's football outfit. Rather bizarrely, she looks great in it.

So we spend the afternoon having fun. Eating a little food, talking, and relaxing, until Brad gets an idea to take some pictures of me. I'm not photogenic and shy away from this type of thing. However, Brad is very persuasive, and so he soon had me stripped down to my boxers, soaking wet from a cold shower, with eight Buddha necklaces around my neck. Brad can make anybody look good, even an old man like me.

Thai Dancer sat there quietly all afternoon. I often caught her looking at me, but I wasn't sure what she was thinking. I had heard stories from Falang who could understand enough Thai to understand what was being said about them behind their back, and it usually wasn't very complimentary. But for some reason, I wasn't convinced that this was the case here.

And after a few hours she asked me to come to her place and meet her friends for a bite to eat. She called a taxi off the street. It was a moped with a Thai man driving. I got on and sat behind the taxi driver while she balanced herself sitting sideways at the back. She put an arm around me, which felt very nice. And then we were off, whizzing down the back streets of Pattaya, far from the usual tourist spots, and very far away from any Falang.

I suddenly thought that here I was, with a bag around my shoulder full of passports, money, two laptops, and an expensive camera. Only a few days earlier an airplane had disappeared en route to China, and there were two people on board who had been travelling on passports that had been stolen in Thailand. So was I being walked into a trap by a beautiful girl. What would be waiting for me when we arrived at her friends' place for dinner.

We arrived, and before I knew it, she had paid the taxi driver. The poor girl with nothing had just paid the taxi driver. Hmmmmm. And she refused to take any money from me.

We went and sat down with her friends, some of whom spoke good English. And we had a dinner of spicy vegetables, some tasty chicken, and Thai whisky. We sat on a patio which adjoined the street. Being the guest, they offered me a cushion to sit on. It was emblazoned with the Manchester United logo, and it made me think back to the time when I had met Sir Alex Ferguson in a hotel lobby, and thought about how far the brand that he built had travelled. I also noticed that their neighbour was ironing some clothes on a towel spread out on the patio floor. I wondered if the clothes belonged to her or if she was doing it for a falang to make some money. I suspect it was the latter.

After that she took me to her little room where she took a shower and got her clothes ready for work. I noticed the pictures of her two children, the same children I had seen on her Facebook page.

After that we were off. Another moped taxi ride back to Brad's, and she paid again. No discussion possible. Total dignity. Wow. I was blown away. We had another hour or so at Brad's. She quietly applied her make-up in readiness for her evening ahead on stage. And then we got another taxi back to town where I picked up my bag, and I dropped her at the entrance to Walking Street, where she was working.

We said a brief goodbye. I thought I caught something in her eye, and for a fleeting moment I thought that she seemed a little upset. But then she was gone. And I didn't look back.

I carried on to the airport with the same taxi and driver. He was an old man from Isan. The same area as Thai Dancer. He told me that while I had been retrieving my bag that they had had time for a chat. And the story that he told me about her was the same one that she had told me. Divorced, two kids, and she supports her entire family because of the lack of rain and poor rice harvest at home.

So it now appeared that she had been telling me the truth all along.

The driver told me that he thought that she was a sincere girl. And that he thought that she liked me. And then he started to sing the English songs that he had learned as a child from a Catholic missionary. His favourite was, "row, row, row your boat, gently down the stream, merrily merrily merrily merrily, life is but a dream". And he said, "that is good song, with much meaning" and he laughed heartily. And then he told me that he was sixty three and that his second wife was thirty-eight. He looked no older than forty. He then said that the secret to looking young is not to take life too seriously.

I thought that this man might be a relative of the Dalai Lama; his wisdom was so profound and so simple.

En route to Bangkok I receive a text message from her. By this time she is probably about to go on stage to perform in her underwear in front of three hundred intoxicated falang. I thought, wow, she must really hate us. A reserved, dignified, and quietly proud woman forced by economic necessity to sell her body in order to support her family.

Her text said "I think that you take care of yourself. Good luck". I knew what she meant. I sent her a nice reply, and then she texted me "I will not forget you. I hope to see you again, Have a safe journey. Love you too".

There I was, sitting in the back seat of a taxi en route from Pattaya to Bangkok, I receive a couple of nice text messages from a girl I don't know and can hardly communicate with, and as a result I break down and cry.

Now I am not a man to cry easily.

And yet, this little dark skinned woman had made me cry. I had to think about it for a little while. She had clearly touched me. And touched a part that had been off limits for some time.

It was at that moment that I knew for sure that all the stories I had heard were true, and that the basis for this book was sound, and that so many sophisticated, educated, and urbane women that I knew living back in the western world could benefit from whatever it was that some of these women living on the other side of the world could manage to do so easily.

After all, if an uneducated, poor woman ten minutes out of the rice fields that run along the Thai Cambodian border, with virtually no ability to speak English, could touch me in this way after just a few days of kindness and attention, then surely there was something to be learned about her method.

And if my friend Brad, the photographer, could find himself madly in love with Suzanna, the Thai girl clad entirely in football gear, four weeks after meeting her, then I knew I was right.

Sure, these women were attractive, but they were hardly classic examples of beauty as defined by western standards, and so it wasn't their looks that were doing it. Nope. It was something else.

Brad makes very interesting videos of himself and his travels about Thailand. They range from elephants walking down the road, street musicians from Isan, to movies of his girlfriend eating dinner at home. Go to his website, bradkoevner.com, and take a look.

He showed me a video of himself and his Suzanna which was very revealing. It is a simple scene where they are preparing and then eating a meal together in his apartment in the Dark Side of Pattaya, the area reserved for locals. The video showed his girlfriend exhibiting a sweet side to her that would beguile any man. She was feminine, and caring, and considerate, and she showed it. And Brad, who has worked with the most beautiful women in the world, was certainly beguiled by her. He was madly in love, and he had only known her for a few weeks.

And I was starting to realize that I was about two or three more meetings with Thai Dancer away from being there myself.

Analyzing it, what had she done? She'd been bold and approached me in the first instance. The sex had happened fast, and it was good. She's then followed up with more attention, and even when she was initially rebuffed, she'd tried again. Despite the fact that she was from nowhere and had nothing, on that last night in Pattaya with me, which had not been planned, she turned up dressed to kill. I caught her looking at me several times during that evening with the Thai dancing, and it was the right type of look, the look of longing and adoration. She went home with me again, and again the sex was good. In fact, it was better than good, it was great, real porn star style stuff. The following day, when she could easily have gone home to rest up for her work night ahead, she chose instead to spend the day with me. And she did what I wanted and needed to do. She joined in, she didn't complain, and she was fun to be with. And somehow, the little minx managed to pay for two taxi rides, invite me for dinner with her and her friends, and show me her little room where she lives. She had even asked me to visit her little village with her. The one where her kids and parents lived. And all that happened in less than twenty-four hours.

Throw in an almost tearful goodbye, and a couple of text messages an hour later and I was done for. On the very brink of being in love. This girl had somehow, and without me even noticing, made it all about me. I realized that no woman back in my world had made me feel as good as this lady had made me feel in a very long time. And as a consequence, I was practically in love with her. No doubt about it. Suddenly I missed her, and I was thinking of ways to show her. Perhaps I could get her a bottle of Chanel and send it to her as a belated Birthday present.

And then I thought about what I had missed out on as a result of being too worried about getting ripped off by the Mamasan.

As Mark Twain said, I was suddenly regretting something that I hadn't done.

But back to the analysis of how she and Suzanna had managed to beguile Brad and myself in such a short period of time. How could it be possible. We were in charge all along, surely. And the girls from the rice paddies were just along for the ride. Right?

Wrong again, Blake.

The explanation was simple. They had turned on the charm in the right way and at the same time, and they hadn't put a foot wrong, not even once. And they had made us feel special. And we learned to like the way that felt pretty darn fast. And we wanted more of it.

Brad was bending over backwards to do anything for Suzanna in order for her to stick around. She now had free accommodation in his apartment. Of course she helped out by keeping the place clean, but still, she was the one in the driving seat, not Brad.

I realized that my behaviour had changed towards my girl too. Whereas a few days earlier I had shown her the door when she asked me for 700 baht, I had voluntarily given her over 10,000 baht in my last day with her. The going rate in Pattaya for the evening that we had enjoyed was 1,500 baht. I gave her 5,000 in the morning. When she stuck around for the afternoon I pushed another 3,000 baht into her hand. I then gave her 500 baht for the taxi rides that she had paid for, plus an additional 2,000 baht when she got out of the taxi and said goodbye. And I was now wishing that I had given her more. Maybe if I had given her another 20,000 baht then she would be spared the indignity of having to perform in front of a bunch of drunken louts for a few evenings, and she could perhaps go home and visit her children.

And then I realized where I was going. Just like all the other men who visit Pattaya, I had started to succumb to the charm and seductive ways of the lovely ladies from Isan. The ladies who had nothing in their pockets, but had the power of apparent sincerity and generosity of soul, with which they could get anything they wanted from any man on whom they shone their light.

And I started to wonder about my future, and what it might be like with a woman like Thai Dancer, and where it might lead if I let it, if I returned to Pattaya in the near future, and went to look for her.

That smart old taxi driver was laughing when he said "maybe time to start new generation", and I wasn't too sure what he was talking about, and then he said, "You come here find Isan girl and start new generation, ha ha ha ha ha" and then I got it.

He was telling me that she liked me and that if I liked her then I should not think too much, just do it, and live long as a result.

I suppose Tiger Woods' father did exactly that. He met and married his lady from Isan, and as a result the world of golf has never been the same.

Maybe, just maybe, I will do the same, so watch this space. And the mere fact that I am giving it a moment's consideration says it all.

Follow the guidelines outlined in this book and you can get that power too.

Conclusion

Catching the big tuna is easier than it might appear. All of the guidelines laid out in this book are arranged around one over riding strategy which will guarantee success if applied properly. You must treat your man better then he has ever been treated before.

The guidance laid down here can not fail to work because if you do things properly then he will quickly become addicted to the way you make him feel. And once he is used to feeling this way, he will soon be addicted to your love, as he perceives it to be. And when you take it away, he will do anything to get it back. Give you anything, buy you anything, go anywhere you want, and do anything that you desire. You will be in complete control of everything. The guidance in this book gives you that power. How you use it is up to you.

The guidelines set out in this book will work for you as long as you follow them closely. Therefore, the risk is not that you fail to catch your big tuna, but that you get so good at playing the game that you are spoiled for choice. And then the very real prospect that you can never decide when to stop playing becomes the new normal for you. It is as if you were a Russian citizen living under the old Communist regime, which meant that the shops were largely empty, and you woke up one day and you were living in New York City instead of Moscow, and you had everything you could ever dream of available to you in shops like Bergdorf

Goodman and Neiman Marcus. In a similar way you could wake up and suddenly have your choice of men, and it would be a hard choice too, like choosing between a top of the range Mercedes and a Range Rover.

Rock Chick, Fun Girl, and Mystery Lady all have this problem. A nice problem to have, you might think, but the fact is that the years are going by for them too, and they have yet to crystallize a profit from their efforts so far, simply because they have become greedy. They land a tuna, but then they have ambitions to catch a bigger one, and it goes on and on, the tuna they catch is never quite good enough. And so they become trapped by their own success. And with each cycle, there is another explanation to make to the next guy why the previous guys never worked out, and it can begin to stretch one's credibility somewhat if you are hoping to convince the fresh tuna that the problem was always the other guy, and not her.

Hopefully you will be careful not to get greedy too, now that you have the power and knowledge and technique to get virtually any man you want to fall in love with you. So use your new found power wisely.

Oh, and one final rule to remember before you embark on your mission, don't leave this book lying around anywhere that a tuna might find it....

Good luck, and please remember to invite me to the wedding!

ABOUT THE AUTHOR

Blake Lavak was born on a small island in the Pacific Ocean in 1961. He grew up on Long Island, New York, before studying Psychology at The London School of Economics. He then enjoyed a successful career in international finance before founding a consulting company which provides high level talent acquisition services to the hedge fund industry in London and New York.

After his fifteen year marriage ended, Blake embarked on a quest to find his soul mate. He was keen to meet someone from outside his established network of friends, colleagues, and acquaintances. And so he embraced the new technology of the time and tried internet dating, and met many fascinating women as a result. Blake firmly believes that it is better to have loved and lost, and to that end he devoted the next seven years of his life to the quest to find The One.

He ventured out to parts of London and abroad that he'd never been to before, to meet women far removed from his normal social circle. And his life was greatly enriched as a result. But he noticed that a small number of the women that he was meeting had a talent for attracting the most eligible men around, while other women seemed to struggle. He watched carefully, always quietly observing, and grew to understand how some women could be so successful, while others were not.

What he learned during those seven years has been distilled into this book, which is now the practical guide to love for women in the 21st century.

Blake spent several years restoring an old sailboat with the help of some friends, and is now planning to sail around the world.

29579211R00134

Made in the USA
Charleston, SC
17 May 2014